# Case Studies in Preparation for the California Reading Competency Test

## Third Edition

**Joanne Rossi**

Notre Dame de Namur University, Belmont

**Beth Schipper**

California State University, Fullerton

Boston  New York  San Francisco
Mexico City  Montreal  Toronto  London  Madrid  Paris
Hong Kong  Singapore  Tokyo  Cape Town  Sydney

Series Editor: Aurora Martínez Ramos
Editorial Assistant: Lynda Giles
Senior Marketing Manager: Krista Clark
Production Editor: Gregory Erb
Editorial Production Service: Argosy Publishing
Composition Buyer: Linda Cox
Manufacturing Buyer: Linda Morris
Electronic Composition: Argosy Publishing
Cover Designer: Elena Sidorova

For related titles and support materials, visit our online catalog at www.ablongman.com

To obtain permission(s) to use material from this work, please submit a written request to Allyn and Bacon, Permission Department, 75 Arlington Street, Boston, MA 02116 or fax your request to 617-848-7320.

Between the time website information is gathered and then published, it is not unusual for some sites to have closed. Also, the transcription of URLs can result in typographical errors. The publisher would appreciate notification where these errors occur so that they may be corrected in subsequent editions.

**Library of Congress Cataloging-in-Publication Data**
The Library of Congress cataloging in publication data was not available at the time of printing

Printed in the United States of America

10 9 8 7 6 5 4 3 2 1   CIN   10 09 08 07 06

# Dedications

To my loving sister, Dr. Sheila Dempsey, a soon-to-be author in her own right.
From Joan

To my parents and first teachers, Edward and Bette, and to Steven Gallup for his
support and motivation.
From Beth

# Preface

## Case Studies in Reading: Preparation for the California Reading Assessment

## Messages to Our Readers

The book is designed to serve three audiences:

- The preservice teacher/credential candidate
- The college instructor of reading courses
- The inservice teacher in the classroom

## To the Preservice Teacher

The purpose of this book is to provide practice in synthesizing and analyzing assessment and strategies for reading in K-8 classrooms. It is also designed to help you pass the Reading Initiative Competence Assessment (RICA™) administered in the state of California. Although the case studies should aid your study for the RICA™, our hope is that the book will enhance your assessment and instruction, and, as a result, increase your students' learning in your future classroom.

The book is organized into a set of case studies at each grade level, followed by a section to assist you with brainstorming your knowledge as a first step in writing your response in narrative form. This is followed by a section of strategic ideas that you should have covered in writing your plan, as well as a sample narrative. At the end of the book is a bibliography of accessible and reader-friendly texts and other resources that can help you fill in any gaps in your knowledge base.

## To the College Instructor

These case studies are intended to aid students in their preparation for the RICA™, but the studies can also be used to enhance instruction in your reading courses, to foster analysis and discussions, for in-class problem-solving, and for assessing student knowledge. The information from your assessment can assist you when planning your own instruction and, in turn, increase learning in the elementary classrooms in which students will eventually find themselves. The bibliography provides resources for filling in gaps in student knowledge.

The case studies represent all elementary grade levels, the four domains required by the RICA™, and a full range of instructional strategies. Because the RICA™ now focuses on the selection of one or two strengths and weaknesses, and one or two methods of instruction, we focused on one or two strategies in the narrative answer in Domains I through IV. In terms of your instruction, you could ask your students to discuss or write alternative answers to the narrative responses in the book based on the list of brainstormed responses. In the case studies that include all four domains, there are multiple assessments and strategies.

The studies are a compilation of actual profiles of readers in public and private schools in northern, central, and southern California. They also represent a wide diversity of cultures, levels, and skills.

## To the Inservice Teacher in the Classroom

Given the diversity of the elementary classroom, the problems that classroom teachers face, and the increased accountability for student success, these case studies can help illuminate problems and suggest strategies to improve student learning. They also should help you identify the gaps in your own knowledge and give you sources to further assist you in filling those gaps.

## How to Use This Book

Each domain presents case studies that deal with classes, groups, or individuals. We suggest that you read what the domain includes, then read the case study and brainstorm about strengths and needs, and finally identify what strategies you would use for instruction. On the actual RICA™, you will have ample room for these notes. For the cases that require assessment methods, brainstorm some ideas about the assessment tools that you would use, and why. Then you will be ready to compare your ideas with the response ideas we have listed on the subsequent pages. Although the brainstorming list will include multiple strategies or assessments, the exam requires you to select just one or two of these items. [Be advised that the RICA™ answer sheets give you less space for cases in Domains I and IV. Therefore, narratives will be shorter (half a page). For cases in Domains II and III, you may be asked to write in depth about the instructional strategy you chose and the rationale for choosing that strategy (one page).]

Next, you can write a narrative. On the brainstormed list of possible answers, we have highlighted one or two ideas that we feel are crucial to the case. (For the large case that covers Domains I through IV, you will have approximately three pages for your narrative response.) Lastly, you can take a look at the sample narrative that we have included for that case.

## Multiple Choice

Following the case studies for each of the domains are multiple-choice questions based on short scenarios. The answers appear immediately after the questions. Use these to test your knowledge of the content, and also to note any terms you may not know. Put each of these terms on index cards and study them over time. Consult the references listed at the end of the book to clarify a concept or check your reading methods textbook for an explanation. There is also a master list of terms following the bibliography.

## About the Authors

Between them, the authors' experience covers over 60 years in the field of reading and language arts as classroom teachers, reading specialists, curriculum consultants, clinicians, administrators, college professors and administrators, and supervisors of student teachers. In the past 20 years, a major focus of the authors' work has been in the research and instruction of language arts assessment in elementary and high school districts. They are also the authors of the book *Portfolios in the Classrooms: Tools for Learning and Instruction.*

# Domains

## Domain I: Planning and Organizing Reading Instruction Based on Ongoing Assessment

### Content Area 1: Conducting Ongoing Assessment of Reading Development
    1.1   Principles of assessment
    1.2   Assessing reading levels
    1.3   Using and communicating assessment results

### Content Area 2: Planning, Organizing, and Managing Reading Instruction
    2.1   Factors involved in planning reading instruction
    2.2   Organizing and managing reading instruction

## Domain II: Developing Phonological and Other Linguistic Processes Related to Reading

### Content Area 3: Phonemic Awareness
    3.1   Assessing phonemic awareness
    3.2   The role of phonemic awareness
    3.3   Developing phonemic awareness

### Content Area 4: Concepts About Print
    4.1   Assessing concepts about print
    4.2   Concepts about print
    4.3   Letter recognition

### Content Area 5: Systematic, Explicit Phonics and Other Word Identification Strategies
    5.1   Assessing phonics and other word identification strategies
    5.2   Explicit phonics instruction
    5.3   Developing fluency
    5.4   Word identification strategies
    5.5   Sight words
    5.6   Terminology

# I

# Planning and Organizing Reading Instruction Based on Ongoing Assessment

# Domain I
# Fourth Grade Individual

> Mitsy is a second-semester fourth grader who is having difficulty in her class. Mitsy has the potential to do better academically, but she does not enjoy reading. Very often, she does not do the assigned twenty minutes per night of reading. The teacher has gathered the following information. Using this information, determine the student's approximate instructional and independent reading levels. Briefly list two of Mitsy's strengths, two areas in which she needs to improve, and specify what data supported your choices.

Make some notes of your own before turning the page.

**Types of Assessment Tools and Strategies**

_____

_____

_____

_____

_____

_____

_____

_____

_____

_____

**Rationale**

_____

_____

_____

_____

_____

_____

_____

_____

_____

Scores from a standard test:

|  | Percentile | Grade Equivalent |
|---|---|---|
| **Word Attack** | 40th | 3.7 |
| **Reading Vocabulary** | 30th | 3.2 |
| **Passage Comprehension** | 35th | 3.5 |
| **Literal** | 48th | 4.2 |
| **Inference** | 25th | 3.0 |
| **Critical Thinking** | 40th | 3.7 |
| **Main Idea** | 50th | 3.9 |

To determine a student's reading level using an informal reading inventory, use the following standards:

|  | Word Recognition* | Comprehension |
|---|---|---|
| **Independent Level** | 95–99% | 90% or higher |
| **Instructional Level** | 90–95% | 65–90% or higher |
| **Frustration Level** | 90% or lower | lower than 65% |
| **Listening Level** |  | 65–80% or higher |

*Not all errors result in loss of meaning. For example: *the* for *a*, or *house* for *home*, retain the intended meaning.

*Mitsy*

Graded Reading Passages Test: Form D—Narrative                267

**The Promise (4)**

INTRODUCTION: This story is about two girls walking together. Please read to find out what happens to them.

**The Promise**

    Long ago, in a distant land beside the sea, people often spotted mermaids. The mermaids had fantastic treasures.

    Sometimes the mermaids would swim to shore. They would spread their treasures around them on the sand. If anyone came near, however, they would jump back in the sea.

    One day, two little girls walking on a beach spied a mermaid. To their surprise, she did not swim away when she saw them. Instead, she smiled and called them over. She gave each a bundle of treasure. "Do not open them until you get home," she warned. The girls promised not to. Then off they went, happy and excited.

    One girl soon grew impatient. When she was out of sight of the mermaid, she decided to open her gift. To her disappointment, she found only ashes and dust.

    The other girl kept her promise. She did not look inside until she got home. In her bundle she found gold, silver, and sparkling jewels. Her family was delighted, and they never forgot their good fortune.

*R* = repeat
*SC* = self-correct

*dk* = don't know

Copyright © 1997 Allyn & Bacon

From Ezra L. Stieglitz. *The Stieglitz Informal Reading Inventory.* (Second Edition) Boston, Massachusetts: Allyn and Bacon 1997.

## COMPREHENSION CHECK

|  |  | Probed Recall | Free Recall |
|---|---|---|---|
| L 1. | Where does this story take place? | ___ | ✓ |
|  | (by the sea) |  |  |
|  | (on a beach) |  |  |
| L 2. | Who did the little girls see? | ___ | ✓ |
|  | (a mermaid) |  |  |
| L 3. | What did the mermaid give to each girl? | dk | ___ |
|  | (a bundle of treasure) |  |  |
| L 4. | What was the promise both girls made to the mermaid? | ___ | ✓ |
|  | (not to open their bundles of treasure until they got home) |  |  |
| I 5. | How did the girl who opened up the first bundle of treasure feel? | dk | ___ |
|  | (sad) |  |  |
|  | (upset) |  |  |
|  | (disappointed) |  |  |
| C 6. | What is the lesson we can learn from this story? | ✓ | _ _ |
|  | (Accept any logical response, such as "If you keep your promise, many good things will come your way" or "Listen to people and heed their warnings.") |  |  |
| **Total Comprehension Errors** |  | **2** (L & I) | |

*Retell*

The mermaid gave the girls something. I don't know what it was called. When they opened it they found different things.

# Brainstorming Response Ideas

## Strengths

- From the informal individual reading assessment—uses some grapho-phonemic, syntactic, and semantic cues
- Gets the general idea of the story
- Uses initial consonants and blends
- Does some self-correcting
- Remembers some details
- From the standardized test—*relative* strengths are in word attack, answering literal questions (factual or detail questions), Critical Thinking (opinion, application)

## Needs

- Work on blending medial vowels and work on endings
- Guesses without using context clues
- Comprehension skills—reading for meaning (monitoring), consistency in using cue systems, inferential thinking (answering inference questions)
- Vocabulary and structural analysis
- Elaboration in retelling
- Fluency

# Narrative

Mitsy's independent level is approximately third grade; instructional level is early fourth grade. This determination is a result of the miscue analysis that includes both a word recognition score of 94% (12 miscues that resulted in a loss of meaning) and a comprehension score of 66%. These scores fall into the instructional range. These levels are also corroborated by the results of the standardized test. One of Mitsy's strengths is her developing ability to self-correct her miscues, but she needs to use this strategy consistently. A second strength is her knowledge of initial consonants and blends.

Even though she has a general idea of what is happening in the story, Mitsy needs to give more details in her retelling. In the structured format of the questions, she does remember major details. Her average score on the standardized Main Idea subtest supports this analysis. She has some difficulty analyzing unknown words, and she does not consistently use context clues or structural analysis. The miscues that result in a loss of meaning on her informal reading inventory support this finding.

# Domain I
# Second Grade Class

This second grade class is located in an affluent area near many large corporations. Parents volunteer in the classroom on a regular basis. Ninety percent of the parents show up for parent-teacher conferences, and they have high expectations for their children. Due to class size reduction, there are twenty students in the class. It is the first week of school. You need to get to know the strengths and needs of your students in order to plan instruction. What two kinds of assessments would you use to get the most information, and what is the rationale for your choices?

Make some notes of your own before turning the page.

**Types of Assessment Tools and Strategies**

_____

_____

_____

_____

_____

_____

_____

_____

_____

**Rationale**

_____

_____

_____

_____

_____

_____

_____

_____

_____

# Brainstorming Response Ideas

## Types of Assessments
- Informal reading inventories, running records (Clay, 1979), miscue analysis and retellings (Goodman & Burke, 1970) on audiotapes
- Observations using checklists for reading, writing, listening, and speaking behaviors
- Anecdotal records
- Writing samples
- Student interest and strategy inventory
- Student-teacher conferences
- Portfolios (including work from first grade, if possible)

## Rationale
- Based on data about individual strengths and needs
- Span all language arts areas—reading, writing, listening, speaking
- Allow teacher to interact with students on an individual basis
- Allow teacher to see patterns in order to group students
- Performance based in real reading, writing, listening, and speaking situations
- Baseline data provides starting point to show evidence of growth over time
- Ongoing assessment uses multiple measures

# Narrative

The teacher may get baseline information by doing individual assessments utilizing short, graded passages that students read aloud and retell on an audiotape. The teacher can then analyze the miscues and reading behavior, and determine the strengths and needs of each child. During the first few weeks, the teacher may also make observations of reading, writing, listening, and speaking behavior, recording the information on checklists. These assessments provide data about individual strengths and needs, and also allow the teacher to see patterns that facilitate instructional planning for grouping students at different levels of skills and abilities.

# Domain I
# Seventh Grade Class

This class has thirty students from mixed backgrounds and cultures: five Chinese, seven Filipino, ten African American, and eight Caucasian. The school is located in an urban setting, and some students are bussed to the school. Only 25% percent of the students in this class are English Language Learners. What are the components of a balanced, comprehensive reading program?

Make some notes of your own before turning the page.

**Components of a Balanced Reading Program**

_____

_____

_____

_____

_____

_____

_____

_____

_____

_____

_____

_____

_____

_____

_____

_____

_____

_____

_____

_____

_____

_____

# Brainstorming Response Ideas

## Components

- Systematic, explicit, and implicit skills instruction (word analysis, vocabulary, spelling)
- Direct teaching of strategies for narrative and expository text
- Individual conferences with students to talk about strengths, needs, interests, culture, etc.
- Ongoing assessments
- Good literature across genres (such as short stories, novels, and poems)
- Expository text
- Sustained, silent reading (SSR)
- Read-alouds
- Integration of writing and speaking
- Portfolios

# Narrative

The components of a balanced, comprehensive reading program have many facets. One is systematic, explicit, and implicit skills instruction, such as word analysis, vocabulary, and spelling. This approach should be combined with guided reading in small groups. Another component is the direct teaching of strategies for narrative and expository text, such as monitoring for meaning. Another component uses good literature across genres (including short stories, novels, and poems) and expository text. Yet another involves integrating writing and speaking through responses to text. Other components involve teacher read-alouds and silent, sustained reading (SSR). Finally, there needs to be ongoing assessments in the form of informal reading inventories followed by individual conferences with students to talk about strengths, needs, interests, culture, etc.

# Multiple-Choice Questions

### Question 1

Ms. Nguyen believes that she has developed a balanced, comprehensive reading/language arts program for her third graders. She includes instruction in all four language arts (reading, writing, listening, and speaking); instruction based on California Language Arts Content Standards; flexible groupings and differentiated instruction to meet the needs of all learners, including English language learners (ELLs); a mix of skills in decoding and strategies in comprehension; and literature-based instruction. What major component is she missing?

a) scaffolding
b) visual aids
c) oral language development
d) assessment

### Question 2

If Ms. Nguyen chooses to give an informal assessment, which of the following might she choose?

a) CELDT
b) STAR6
c) IRI
d) criterion-referenced test

### Question 3

Mrs. Gomez does an informal reading inventory on each of her students in her seventh grade language core class. What information is she *not* likely to glean from this assessment?

a) information about the student's attitude toward reading
b) information about what decoding and word analysis strategies the student is using
c) information about whether the student is monitoring
d) information about the student's ability to answer the questions about the text

### Question 4

After Mrs. Gomez evaluates the inventory, she discusses the results with each student. What is the main reason for this practice?

a) to correct students' word pronunciations
b) to allow students to communicate the information to their parents
c) to show students where they are weak
d) to make students partners in their reading instruction

## Question 5

Mrs. Gomez also administers a standardized reading test to her students. She needs to interpret the results and communicate them to parents. The results are reported in percentiles. Max's score fell into the 65th percentile for total reading. When Max's parents ask what a percentile is, how should she define it and explain Max's percentile score to his parents?

a) Max is a below-average reader.
b) Max reads better than 65% of the students in seventh grade classes.
c) Max has poor strategies for comprehension.
d) Max's score would be equal to a C or a D on his report card.

## Question 6

Mrs. Fari has a new kindergarten class and needs to obtain some baseline data on her students. One of the assessments will deal with concepts about print. Which of the following would *not* be included in this particular assessment?

a) left-to-right orientation
b) cover of the book
c) word segmentation
d) recognition of a capital letter

## Question 7

Mrs. Fari also needs to assess her students on their phonemic awareness abilities. Which of the following would *not* be included in her assessment in this area?

a) testing the ability to rhyme
b) testing the ability to decode "cat"
c) testing the ability to segment a word orally
d) testing the ability to blend a word orally

## Question 8

Mr. Ortega has a fifth grade class that is very diverse. Half the class consists of English language learners from India, Pakistan, the Philippines, and Mexico, at CELDT Levels 3 and 4. After having three groups for reading in the first two months of the year, the teacher found that half of the students were progressing rapidly in both reading and English language development, some were making moderate progress, and others had made very little growth beyond their baseline levels. How should he manage and organize his classroom for optimal growth?

a) whole-class instruction with scaffolding
b) computer-based instruction for the whole class
c) flexible grouping and differentiated instruction
d) oral instruction in Spanish

## Question 9

Mr. Ortega has a new student from Ethiopia who tested at CELDT Level 1. How should Mr. Ortega plan and manage instruction for this newcomer?

    a) teach the student using grade-level benchmarks

    b) increase volume of speech and speak more slowly

    c) have him join the lowest-level reading group

    d) use differentiated, individualized instruction

# Answers to Multiple-Choice Questions

## Question 1

The answer is *d) assessment*, because without it the teacher will have a difficult time matching the needs of the individual students and the whole group with the instruction that would best serve those needs. Answers a and b are comprehension strategies; oral language development is already embedded under the umbrella of listening and speaking in the category of language arts.

## Question 2

The answer is *c) IRI* (informal reading inventory), because it is the only choice that is an informal measure and somewhat subjective. CELDT, STAR6, and a criterion-referenced test are all standardized measures.

## Question 3

The answer is *a) information about the student's attitude toward reading*. Although the teacher may have a discussion about the student's attitude toward reading, this information is not automatically embedded in the IRI procedure. All of the other answers contain components of an analysis of student reading behaviors that could be gleaned from an IRI.

## Question 4

The answer is *d) to make students partners in their reading instruction*. In order for students to be engaged in reading and empowered to make progress, they need to understand strategies of good readers that they are already using, and what kinds of skills and strategies they need to work on in collaboration with their teacher. Answer a is not part of this process. Answer b may happen, but it is not the main reason the teacher holds the conference. Answer c is only a part of the process, but not the main reason for the conference.

## Question 5

The answer is *b) Max reads better than 65% of the students in seventh grade classes*. Answer a is incorrect because the score tells that Max is an above-average reader. Answer c is incorrect because we would need more data to confirm this response, and it is unlikely given his percentile score. Answer d is also unlikely, and even though a student's percentile score might reflect his performance in the classroom, standardized tests are not used to determine a student's grade on a report card.

## Question 6

The answer is *c) word segmentation*, which is a component of phonemic awareness, not concepts about print. The others are all under the umbrella of concepts about print that include reading from left to right, identifying the cover of the book, and the recognition of a capital letter.

## Question 7

The answer is *b) testing the ability to decode "cat."* The ability to decode "cat" falls into the realm of phonics, because "cat" is presented in written form and requires an understanding of the alphabetic principle. The other choices—rhyming, blending, and segmenting—are all orally presented and belong to the category of phonemic awareness.

## Question 8

The answer is *c) flexible grouping and individualized instruction*. Giving whole-class instruction, even with scaffolding, does not meet the needs of all students. The same is true for answers b and d.

## Question 9

The answer is *d) use differentiated, individualized instruction*, because this student is just beginning to learn English—his needs are very different from all the other students. Therefore, he would not be able to join a group or to meet any benchmarks at the fifth grade level. Speaking loudly in a language the student does not understand does nothing to further development—there is nothing wrong with his hearing.

# II Developing Phonological and Other Linguistic Processes Related to Reading

# Domain II
## Second Grade Individual

Carmen is a first grade English language learner at CELDT Level 2. She attends an ESL class for an hour each day. In her regular classroom, she tends to be shy, but she will risk giving some answers. When she is around children on the playground who also speak Spanish but have more control of English (CELDT Level 3), she is bubbly, outgoing, and can carry on a conversation in English with relative ease. She is already fluent in her native Spanish, but she is making progress in speaking English in the ESL class. She has some phonemic awareness in terms of rhyme and segmenting. She is able to write her name and draw a picture of a person. The school district has mandated a scripted program in reading. However, at this point, she does not understand the overall process of reading. Using this information as well as the two following sample assessments, list two of Carmen's strengths and two of her needs, and select two additional instructional strategies beyond the scripted phonics program that you would use with Carmen. Explain how you would implement these strategies.

## Checklist for Observing Concepts about Print

| NAME | | | | | | | | | | | | | | | |
|---|---|---|---|---|---|---|---|---|---|---|---|---|---|---|---|
| Carmen | | | | | | | | | | | | | | | |
| Time at school | 2 yrs. | | | | | | | | | | | | | | |
| Front of book | — | | | | | | | | | | | | | | |
| Print contains message | ✓ | | | | | | | | | | | | | | |
| Where to start | ✓ | | | | | | | | | | | | | | |
| Left to right | ✓ | | | | | | | | | | | | | | |
| Return sweep | ✓ | | | | | | | | | | | | | | |
| Word by word matching | ✓ | | | | | | | | | | | | | | |
| First and last | ✓ | | | | | | | | | | | | | | |
| Print is right way up | ✓ | | | | | | | | | | | | | | |
| Left page before right | ✓ | | | | | | | | | | | | | | |
| Full stop | — | | | | | | | | | | | | | | |
| Question mark | — | | | | | | | | | | | | | | |
| Capital and lower case letter correspondence | — | | | | | | | | | | | | | | |
| Letters | ✓ | | | | | | | | | | | | | | |
|    Recognizes difference/ knows the term. | — | | | | | | | | | | | | | | |
| Words | — | | | | | | | | | | | | | | |
| First and last letters of words | — | | | | | | | | | | | | | | |
| Capital letters | — | | | | | | | | | | | | | | |
| Comments | | | | | | | | | | | | | | | |

This page is copyright-free.

### Legend

| | |
|---|---|
| ✓ | **knows** |
| 0 | **does not know** |
| — | **does not know** |
| 0✓ | **corrected by student** |

*Table 5.1* **Alphabet Recognition Test**   Carmen

A✓  S✓  D✓  F  (G)  H✓  (J)

(K)  (L✓)  (P̃ᴮ✓)  O✓  I✓  (U)  (Y✓)

T✓  R✓  E  (W)  Q̇  Z✓  X✓

(C)  (V)  P̃B  (N)  (M)

a✓  s✓  d✓  f  (g)  h✓  jⁱ

(k)  lⁱ  p✓  o✓  iⁱ  hu  (y)

t✓  (r)  (e)  (w)  (q)  (z)  x✓

c✓  (y)  b✓  ʰn  ʷm  a✓  (y)

(g)  ᵈq  t✓  a✓  (g)  t✓  (q)

From Margaret Ann Richek, et al. *Reading Problems: Assessment and Teaching Strategies* (Third Edition) Needham, Massachusetts: Allyn and Bacon. 1996

Make some notes of your own before turning the page.

## Strengths

_____
_____
_____
_____
_____
_____
_____
_____
_____

## Needs

_____
_____
_____
_____
_____
_____
_____
_____
_____

## Strategies

_____
_____
_____
_____
_____
_____
_____
_____
_____

# Brainstorming Response Ideas

## Strengths

- Is verbal in Spanish, her native language
- Is progressing in English language development
- Has some concepts of print in place
- Can draw a picture of a person
- Knows some alphabet letters
- Can communicate at basic English level
- Is able to write her name
- Has some good social skills

## Needs

- English language development (vocabulary and syntax)
- Phonemic awareness
- Additional concepts of print
- Sight words
- Systematic phonics, spelling patterns
- Environmental print
- An understanding of the process of reading

## Strategies

- Additional practice with phonemic awareness—poems, rhymes, chants, and choral reading
- Alphabet presented in different contexts
- Sight words
- Language Experience Approach using stories dictated by the student so that she can connect what she is saying with written text and better understand the process of reading
- Oral cloze—read-alouds in the context of shared reading, with certain words supplied by the student
- Spelling practice with consonant-vowel-consonant (*cvc*) pattern and beyond (for example, *cvce*), journal writing, dictation, word wall, and individual dictionary
- Teacher read-alouds of quality literature
- Daily independent reading of student's own Language Experience stories

## Narrative

Based on her fluency in Spanish, Carmen has strengths in her native language, and some knowledge of print and print concepts. She is an emergent reader in a school with a mandated, scripted reading program that emphasizes explicit, systematic phonics and decodable text. This program alone is not meeting her needs. Carmen still needs vocabulary and syntax development along with a better understanding of the reading process through authentic connected text.

Carmen needs to continue instruction in phonemic awareness, letter recognition, and concepts of print. However, two additional strategies could be integrated to address Carmen's needs. The first strategy is the use of teacher read-alouds/think-alouds to allow her to learn more about English syntax and the vocabulary. The second strategy, which incorporates many of the components for emergent readers, is the Language Experience Approach. The first step is for the teacher to read a picture book to Carmen and other children at her level. Following the reading, the teacher and the students discuss the story. After a full discussion, students dictate what they would like to say about the story. The teacher writes their words verbatim on a chart paper, and this becomes the text for reading. The teacher uses the difficult words embedded in the text to teach phonics and sight vocabulary. The teacher and the students read the text several times together. This process continues with new dictated stories until students are ready to transition to actual books. These integrated strategies can serve both of Carmen's primary needs.

# Domain II
# Third Grade Group

This third grade class has a high percentage of students in Title I. For the most part, they all speak English. Few of the children are read to at home, but all enjoy story time when the teacher reads to them. They respond to the stories through discussions. They also enjoy independent reading, when they look at or read a book by themselves. Four of the students are in the emergent reader stage. They know some sight words, but they read word-by-word, and therefore, reading is laborious. Reading and phonics analysis shows that they know most initial consonant sounds and use those to randomly guess at words, but they ignore ending consonants and medial vowels. Both writing and spelling are on a lower developmental level: the beginning of first grade, phonetic stage. State two strengths and two needs of this group. What two instructional strategies would you provide for these students?

Make some notes of your own before turning the page.

## Strengths

_____
_____
_____
_____
_____

## Needs

_____
_____
_____
_____
_____

## Strategies

_____
_____
_____
_____
_____

# Brainstorming Response Ideas

## Strengths

- Know some sight words
- Know most consonant sounds
- Have an interest in reading
- Have some comprehension of what they are reading

## Needs

- Phonics skills on an automatic level to promote fluency and comfort with reading
- Strategies to retain sight words
- Strategies for monitoring and self-correction
- Strategies for spelling

## Strategies

- Give opportunities to apply phonics skills using contexts such as decodable or predictable texts during shared reading.
- Based on needs, do direct and systematic instruction in phonics with emphasis on word families—for example, onsets and rimes, blending, vowels, digraphs, and syllables.
- Create activity centers that provide practice in phonics skills and previously taught generalizations.
- Give direct instruction in strategies for monitoring and self-correction in reading—for example, using picture and context clues to support grapho-phonemic elements.
- Use the language Experience Approach with follow-up mini-lessons on word patterns that present difficulties.
- Introduce choral reading to promote word recognition and fluency.
- Add think-alouds to read-alouds, where teacher models how good readers process text as they read.
- Send books home that students have practiced and have them share them with their parents, to encourage home or family literacy involvement.
- Provide opportunities for writing authentic pieces every day (writing that is purposeful and meaningful).
- Provide opportunities for interactive writing with students and teacher (shared pen, shared writing).
- Put up word walls that contain the most frequently used words (sight words); students can add to the wall and refer to it when writing.
- Have individual student-made dictionaries.

- Use sight words from the word wall to have students make cards that contain the words that the individual is struggling with; students can review cards each day and practice using visual, auditory, tactile, and kinesthetic modes (VAKT) so that the student sees the word, listens to the sounds in the word, writes the word, and then traces each letter with a finger to get the "feel" of the word.
- Conduct individual reading and writing conferences with the student to nurture strengths and support weak areas.

## Narrative

This third grade group has some relative strengths in the areas of knowledge of initial consonants and sight words. However, they are still in need of decoding strategies involving medial and ending consonants and a larger cadre of sight words. By third grade—and if this group has had a continuous phonics program from the beginning of school—instruction should emphasize word families rather than individual phonemes. This approach still utilizes systematic direct instruction in phonics, but the focus is on word patterns. For example, if the pattern is *ack*, students learn to build words using that pattern: *j/ack*, *t/ack*, *sh/ack*. Students need instruction and practice in how to blend the onset with the rime. Then they need to be taught to determine whether the word is one they recognize from speech, and they need to check to see whether the word makes sense in the context of the sentence.

To address the lack of sight words, the teacher can select the sight words from the word wall that each individual student needs. Students then make cards that contain the words. The student reviews the cards each day and practices using visual, auditory, kinesthetic, and tactile modes (VAKT) to see the word, listen to the sounds in the word, write the word, and then trace each letter with a finger to get the "feel" of the word. This practice greatly increases the chances that the student will get the words into memory.

# Domain II
# First Grade Group

In this first grade class, various Asian languages and cultures are represented. Students are all second-generation Americans and English-proficient. It is September, and many of the students can read simple, decodable text that follows predictable patterns with high-frequency sight words. However, four of the students are new to the school and are nonreaders and nonwriters. They are reluctant to take any risks in either speaking or writing. What three assessment strategies might this teacher employ to determine his or her plan of instruction for these students, and why would the teacher use these particular methods?

Make some notes of your own before turning the page.

## Assessments and Rationale

_____

_____

_____

_____

_____

_____

_____

_____

_____

_____

_____

_____

_____

_____

_____

_____

_____

# Brainstorming Response Ideas

## Types of Assessments and Rationale

- Concepts of print—shows book handling, left-to-right and top and bottom (directionality) orientation, upper- and lowercase letter recognition, one-to-one letter and word correspondence, tracking, realization that print is speech written down, knowledge of punctuation and capitalization
- Phonemic awareness test (the stage prior to phonics instruction)—verbal assessment tests students' knowledge that words are made up of individual sounds (phonemes), whether they are able to blend sounds together to make syllables and words (sound blending), whether they are able to break words down (segmention), whether they are able to make substitutions and deletions using onsets and rimes
- Listening samples with retelling—assess students' ability to remember, understand, and sequence a story
- Observations and anecdotal records—detail and document benchmarks and developmental milestones in listening and speaking
- Sight word assessment—gauge whether students have visual memory for sight vocabulary (Dolch words)
- Individual conferences—find out about family literacy history, such as whether students are read to at home; what language is spoken by parents; whether parents are readers; how much television students watch; student's interests; extent of outside activities, such as additional instruction in their native language, ballet, music, soccer, or art classes

# Narrative

The following measures will yield information about a student's readiness to read. A concepts-about-print test will give the teacher an idea of how familiar students are with books in general. This kind of assessment shows book handling, directionality, upper- and lowercase letter recognition, one-to-one letter and word correspondence, tracking, realization that print is speech written down, and knowledge of punctuation and capitalization.

A phonemic awareness test might be used to determine whether students know that words are made up of phonemes, whether students can identify rhymes, whether they are able to blend and segment sounds, and whether they can make substitutions and deletions using onsets and rimes. Because this is an auditory set of tasks, students should have some knowledge of sounds and sound manipulation as a prerequisite to phonics.

Because listening samples with retelling equate to a student's potential level in reading, listening samples can be used to assess students' ability to remember, understand, and sequence a story.

These three assessments can give developmental information that would allow the teacher to assess strengths and needs and inform instruction for each student.

# Domain II
# Kindergarten Class

In this first-semester kindergarten class, there are twenty students. Twenty-five percent have Spanish as their first language, and 25% have Tagalog as their primary language (eight have limited English and two are non-English-speaking). The other 50% are English speaking. There is a mixture of socioeconomic levels; many students are bussed in from outlying rural areas. Two-thirds of the students have had no preschool experiences. Using this information and the following sample assessments, identify some strengths that the majority of students have in common, identify two categories of needs of the group, and name three major instructional strategies you would use with this class.

Make some notes of your own before turning the page.

## Strengths

_____

_____

_____

_____

_____

## Needs

_____

_____

_____

_____

_____

## Strategies

_____

_____

_____

_____

_____

## Checklist for Observing Concepts about Print

**NAME**

Minna L.

| | | | | | | | | |
|---|---|---|---|---|---|---|---|---|
| Time at school | Big | | | | | | | |
| Front of book | ✓ | | | | | | | |
| Print contains message | — | | | | | | | |
| Where to start | — | | | | | | | |
| Left to right | — | | | | | | | |
| Return sweep | — | | | | | | | |
| Word by word matching | — | | | | | | | |
| First and last | — | | | | | | | |
| Print is right way up | — | | | | | | | |
| Left page before right | — | | | | | | | |
| Full stop | — | | | | | | | |
| Question mark | — | | | | | | | |
| Capital and lower case letter correspondence | — | | | | | | | |
| Letters — Recognizes difference/knows the term. | ✓— | | | | | | | |
| Words | | | | | | | | |
| First and last letters of words | — | | | | | | | |
| Capital letters | — | | | | | | | |
| Comments | | | | | | | | |

This page is copyright-free

Knows a few letters.
(all Capitals)

Minna L.

### Listening & Speaking Asset Sheet

Name _Minna L._    Grade _K_  Year _199-_
(circle)    NEP (LEP) ESL

| | 1st Date | 2nd Date |
|---|---|---|
| **Comprehension** | | |
| Can tell the difference | | |
| between words | ✓ | ____ |
| Gains understanding | | |
| when spoken to | ✓ | ____ |
| when read to | ✓ | ____ |
| Can hold information in memory | ✓— | ____ |
| Is able to follow directions | | |
| one step | ✓ | ____ |
| two step | = | ____ |
| three or more steps | = | ____ |
| **Expression** | | |
| Speaks clearly | ✓— | ____ |
| Uses language appropriately | | |
| in social situations | ✓— | ____ |
| Uses vocabulary appropriate to age | | |
| in classroom | ✓— | ____ |
| Uses standard English grammar | = | ____ |
| Uses standard native language | ✓ | ____ |
| Can retell a story | = | ____ |
| in sequence | | ____ |
| with major details | | ____ |
| Can label and categorize | | |
| things | — | ____ |
| ideas | . | ____ |
| Communicates meaningful ideas | ✓— | ____ |
| Participates in discussions | ✓— | ____ |
| Responses to questions | | |
| in organized manner | ____ | ____ |
| on factual level | ____ | ____ |
| on inferential level | ____ | ____ |
| on critical thinking level | ____ | ____ |
| Uses language to solve problems | ____ | ____ |

© Joanne Rossi & Beth Schipper, 1994

**Checklist for Observing Concepts about Print**

NAME *Benny D.*

| | | | | | | | | | | | |
|---|---|---|---|---|---|---|---|---|---|---|---|
| Time at school | Beg. | | | | | | | | | | |
| Front of book | ✓ | | | | | | | | | | |
| Print contains message | ✓ | | | | | | | | | | |
| Where to start | ✓ | | | | | | | | | | |
| Left to right | — | | | | | | | | | | |
| Return sweep | — | | | | | | | | | | |
| Word by word matching | — | | | | | | | | | | |
| First and last | — | | | | | | | | | | |
| Print is right way up | — | | | | | | | | | | |
| Left page before right | ✓ | | | | | | | | | | |
| Full stop | — | | | | | | | | | | |
| Question mark | | | | | | | | | | | |
| Capital and lower case letter correspondence | — | | | | | | | | | | |
| Letters | | | | | | | | | | | |
| Recognizes difference | ✓ | | | | | | | | | | |
| knows the term | — | | | | | | | | | | |
| Words | | | | | | | | | | | |
| First and last letters of words | — | | | | | | | | | | |
| Capital letters | — | | | | | | | | | | |
| Comments | | | | | | | | | | | |

This page is copyright-free

*Can recognize most letters - upper and lower*

**Listening & Speaking Asset Sheet**

Name *Benny D.*   Grade *K*   Year *199—*

(circle)   NEP   LEP   (ESL)

| | 1st Date | 2nd Date |
|---|---|---|
| **Comprehension** | | |
| Can tell the difference | | |
|     between words | ✓ | ———— |
| Gains understanding | | |
|     when spoken to | ✓ | ———— |
|     when read to | ✓ | ———— |
| Can hold information in memory | ✓ | ———— |
| Is able to follow directions | | |
|     one step | ✓ | ———— |
|     two step | ✓ | ———— |
|     three or more steps | — | ———— |
| **Expression** | | |
| Speaks clearly | ✓— | ———— |
| Uses language appropriately | | |
|     in social situations | ✓— | ———— |
| Uses vocabulary appropriate to age | | |
|     in classroom | ✓— | ———— |
| Uses standard English grammar | ✓— | ———— |
| Uses standard native language | ✓ | ———— |
| Can retell a story | ✓ | ———— |
|     in sequence | ✓ | ———— |
|     with major details | ✓ | ———— |
| Can label and categorize | | |
|     things | ✓ | ———— |
|     ideas | | ———— |
| Communicates meaningful ideas | ✓— | ———— |
| Participates in discussions | ✓— | ———— |
| Responses to questions | | |
|     in organized manner | | ———— |
|     on factual level | ✓ | ———— |
|     on inferential level | | ———— |
|     on critical thinking level | | ———— |
| Uses language to solve problems | | ———— |

Joanne Rossi & Beth Schipper, 1994

August

Benny D.

## Checklist for Observing Concepts about Print

NAME
Alviar F.

| | Beg. |
|---|---|
| Time at school | Beg. |
| Front of book | ✓ |
| Print contains message | — |
| Where to start | — |
| Left to right | — |
| Return sweep | — |
| Word by word matching | — |
| First and last | — |
| Print is right way up | |
| Left page before right | |
| Full stop | |
| Question mark | |
| Capital and lower case letter correspondence | — |
| Letters | |
| Recognizes difference/ knows the term | — |
| Words | |
| First and last letters of words | — |
| Capital letters | — |
| Comments | |

This page is copyright-free

Cannot recognize letters by name yet.

August

Alviar F.

## Listening & Speaking Asset Sheet

Name Alviar F.   Grade K  Year 199–

(circle)   NEP (LEP) ESL

| | 1st Date | 2nd Date |
|---|---|---|
| **Comprehension** | | |
| Can tell the difference | | |
| between words | ✓– | |
| Gains understanding | | |
| when spoken to | ✓ | |
| when read to | ✓ | |
| Can hold information in memory | — | |
| Is able to follow directions | | |
| one step | — | |
| two step | | |
| three or more steps | | |
| **Expression** | | |
| Speaks clearly | ✓– | |
| Uses language appropriately | | |
| in social situations | ✓– | |
| Uses vocabulary appropriate to age | | |
| in classroom | ✓– | |
| Uses standard English grammar | — | |
| Uses standard native language | ✓ | |
| Can retell a story | — | |
| in sequence | — | |
| with major details | — | |
| Can label and categorize | | |
| things | — | |
| ideas | — | |
| Communicates meaningful ideas | | |
| Participates in discussions | ✓– | |
| Responses to questions | | |
| in organized manner | | |
| on factual level | ✓ | |
| on inferential level | | |
| on critical thinking level | | |
| Uses language to solve problems | | |

© Joanne Rossi & Beth Schipper, 1994

**Checklist for Observing Concepts about Print**

NAME

*Rena P.*

| | |
|---|---|
| Time at school | Beg |
| Front of book | ✓ |
| Print contains message | ✓ |
| Where to start | — |
| Left to right | — |
| Return sweep | — |
| Word by word matching | — |
| First and last | — |
| Print is right way up | — |
| Left page before right | — |
| Full stop | — |
| Question mark | — |
| Capital and lower case letter correspondence | — |
| Letters | |
|   Recognizes difference | — |
|   Knows the term | |
| Words | — |
| First and last letters of words | — |
| Capital letters | — |
| Comments | — |

This page is copyright-free

*Knows about 10 letters – upper case*

**Listening & Speaking Asset Sheet**

Name  *Rena P.*  Grade  K  Year  199-

(circle)   NEP   LEP   (ESL)

| | 1st Date | 2nd Date |
|---|---|---|
| **Comprehension** | | |
| Can tell the difference | | |
|   between words | ✓ | |
| Gains understanding | | |
|   when spoken to | ✓ | |
|   when read to | ✓ | |
| Can hold information in memory | — | |
| Is able to follow directions | | |
|   one step | ✓ | |
|   two step | ✓ | |
|   three or more steps | — | |
| **Expression** | | |
| Speaks clearly | ✓ | |
| Uses language appropriately | | |
|   in social situations | ✓– | |
| Uses vocabulary appropriate to age | | |
|   in classroom | ✓– | |
| Uses standard English grammar | ✓– | |
| Uses standard native language | ✓ | |
| Can retell a story | — | |
|   in sequence | — | |
|   with major details | — | |
| Can label and categorize | | |
|   things | ✓ | |
|   ideas | ✓ | |
| Communicates meaningful ideas | ✓ | |
| Participates in discussions | ✓ | |
| Responses to questions | | |
|   in organized manner | | |
|   on factual level | ✓ | |
|   on inferential level | — | |
|   on critical thinking level | — | |
| Uses language to solve problems | — | |

© Joanne Rossi & Beth Schipper, 1994

August

*Rena P.*

# Brainstorming Response Ideas

## Strengths

- Most students can understand some spoken English.
- All students can express themselves in their native language.
- Three out of four students can follow simple, one-step directions.
- All students can use some English to express themselves.
- Three out of four students can communicate meaningful ideas.
- All students can take part in discussions, to some extent.
- Three out of four students can draw a recognizable person.
- Three out of four students can answer simple fact-based questions.

## Needs

- To be able to follow two- and three-step directions; continue development in English language and syntax, including listening skills and expressive language; develop categorizing skills; develop and extend memory skills
- To have groundwork for reading, including phonemic awareness, letter and letter-sound recognition, structure of text (words and sentences), immersion in print, concepts about print, word recognition

## Strategies

- Teach concepts about print using read-alongs using predictable text (text with repetitive patterns), modeling directionality (the left-to-right orientation of text), word-by-word matching, tracking across the page, stopping at the ends of sentences.
- Immerse the classroom environment in print; label corners of the room and objects around the room; implement shared reading and writing through practice with daily messages (days of the week, months of the year, weather for the day, events at school, etc.).
- Give students practice activities that involve visual recognition of shapes and names of alphabet letters through various hands-on activities (tactile/kinesthetic), such as magnetic letters, felt boards, games, etc.
- Practice the sounds of word patterns through chanting, choral reading, and rhymes in poetry.
- Practice oral cloze (during choral reading, stop just before a word and ask class to tell what the next word will be; in the beginning of this activity, use words with rhyming pattern); this activity shows students that print has meaning.

## Narrative

From the attached assessments, it appears that most students can understand some spoken English. All students can express themselves in their native language. Knowing another language is a strength, because it means that students have some background in a language structure, even if it is not English. Therefore, they all are beginning to express themselves in simple English, participate to some extent in discussions, and answer factual questions. Three out of four students can draw a recognizable person, so they can show the ability to conceptualize, and use their fine-motor skills.

This group has several needs that center on language development and emergent reading. In particular, these students need to continue to develop listening and expressive skills in English, categorizing, and memory skills in order to follow directions in class. They also need to have more groundwork for reading in the form of concepts about print, phonemic awareness, letter and sound recognition, knowledge of text structure, and word recognition.

In particular, this kindergarten group needs extensive work with strategies to expand their concepts about print (directionality, word-by-word matching, tracking, and so on) through direct instruction and read-alongs using predictable text. They need a classroom immersed in print: corners of the room and objects around the room should be labeled, and practice with shared reading and writing through daily messages (days of the week, months of the year, weather for the day, events at school, etc.) should be implemented. Students also need practice in the visual recognition of shapes and names of alphabet letters and, eventually, word recognition, through various hands-on activities (tactile/kinesthetic), such as magnetic letters, felt boards, games, and the like. They can practice the sounds of word patterns through chanting, choral reading, and rhymes. They should also practice oral cloze during choral reading, to show that print has meaning.

# Multiple-Choice Questions

### Question 1
Mrs. Watkins's second grade reading group has some difficulty applying phonics strategies. Out of the following phonics generalizations, rules, and components, which one would be the least useful?
a) *r*-controlled vowel
b) *ch* as it is pronounced in "kitchen"
c) silent *gh* is silent as it is in "night"
d) phonogram *ie* as it is pronounced in "field"

In his kindergarten class, Mr. Gonzales has many students who are not yet readers. Use this information to answer the following three questions.

### Question 2
Mr. Gonzales is reading an example of predictable text. Which of the following is an example of what he might be reading?
a) Once upon a time, a troll wandered the woods in search of gold.
b) *Brown Bear, Brown Bear, What Do You See?*
c) Pat has a cat that sits on a mat.
d) There was an old woman who lived in a shoe; she had so many children she didn't know what to do.

### Question 3
Mr. Gonzales also does phonemic awareness activities on a daily basis. Which of the following phonemic awareness activities would be considered the lowest level of difficulty?
a) segmentation
b) blending
c) rhyming
d) substitutions/additions/deletions

### Question 4
In addition to teaching phonemic awareness activities, Mr. Gonzales is going to introduce letter and sound recognition. Which of the following strategies and principles would this activity be the beginning of?
a) onsets and rimes.
b) blends.
c) the alphabetic principle.
d) Elkonin boxes.

### Question 5

In her first grade class, Ms. Haddad used sentence strips in a pocket chart to present the verse "Peter Piper picked a peck of pickled peppers," which she had students chant. She then asked students to tell what they noticed about the sentence. What type of instruction is this an example of?

    a) differentiated instruction
    b) implicit or embedded phonics
    c) explicit, systematic phonics
    d) structural analysis

### Question 6

On another day, Ms. Haddad used Lesson 5 from the teacher's manual to reinforce the "p" in the initial consonant position. First, she told students that they would be working on the letter "p." She showed them the letter "p" on a card and discussed what sound it makes in the initial position. Students had a slate board and chalk. They divided their slate into four sections, each section containing a word family such as _ot, _at, _ill, and _al. Ms. Haddad said the word "pat" and students filled in the initial consonant in the blank space. She then asked students to hold up their slates to check their work. What type of instruction is this an example of?

    a) explicit, systematic phonics
    b) implicit, embedded phonics
    c) structural analysis
    d) differentiated instruction

### Question 7

Mrs. Lee has a fifth grade group; her assessment determined that they have fluency problems. Which of the following would *not* be an effective strategy for Mrs. Lee to use to increase their fluency?

    a) having the students point to each word as they read
    b) having them do repeated readings of the same text
    c) increasing speed of word recognition
    d) implementing daily independent reading time (SSR, DEAR)

### Question 8

Mrs. Lee has another group that needs work in structural analysis. Which of the following words would best lend itself to this skill?

    a) preconceived
    b) laugh
    c) mountains
    d) decided

## Question 9

In her writer's workshop, Mrs. Lee noticed that students needed work on spelling. Which of the following strategies would be the *least* effective in supporting students in spelling?

    a) dictionary use
    b) word walls
    c) frequent practice in writing and proofreading
    d) class spelling tests

## Question 10

Ms. Latsy has a third grade class in which students are at different stages of writing. What stage of spelling is demonstrated by this sample: "The siup canot flote in the watr" (the ship cannot float in the water)?

    a) transitional
    b) pre-phonetic
    c) phonetic
    d) semi-phonetic

# Answers to Multiple-Choice Questions

## Question 1

The answer is *d) phonogram* ie *as it is pronounced in "field,"* as this is a phonics rule that has the most exceptions (17% utility). The other generalizations or rules have much higher percentages of usefulness or utility: answer a has 78% utility, answer b has 95% utility, and answer c has 100% utility (Clymer, 1963).

## Question 2

The answer is *b) Brown Bear, Brown Bear, What Do You See?* because its text contains a predictable pattern that students will be able to recognize and reproduce with practice. Answer a might give students a sense of story, as many stories begin with "Once upon a time," but students don't automatically know what will come next in the story. Answer c is decodable text, one that follows a decodable pattern; in this case, *at*. Answer d is incorrect because although it contains rhyme, students cannot automatically predict the next line.

## Question 3

The answer is *c) rhyming*. According to the progression of difficulty in phonemic awareness, students generally have less difficulty with rhyming than they do with breaking a word down into its phonemes (*pat = p-a-t*, answer a), making a word out of its phonemes (*p-a-t = pat*, answer b), or making new words by substituting letters (*taking away "p" from pat and adding "b" to make bat,* answer d).

## Question 4

The answer is *c) the alphabetic principle,* where students learn letter-sound association. Answers a and b are components of this principle. Answer d is a strategy that teachers might use to demonstrate single phonemes, blends, or digraphs.

## Question 5

The answer is *b) implicit or embedded phonics.* This instruction occurs when the teacher uses the phonetic pattern of the text to teach a lesson on phonics and asks students to find the pattern—in this case, the consonant "p" in the initial position of a word. Answer a does not apply, because there is no evidence that these students were singled out to have this lesson. Answer c is incorrect because this lesson was created using a sentence in which the phonic component was a part; explicit instruction would have included the presentation of the phonetic component in the beginning of the lesson. Answer d has to do with multisyllabic words that lend themselves to an analysis of their roots, suffixes, prefixes, and origin, etc.

## Question 6

The answer is *a) explicit, systematic phonics.* This is an example of a teacher presenting the phonics concept first and giving students guided practice. The explanations for Question 5 apply here as well.

## Question 7

The answer is *a) having the students point to each word as they read,* because by the time students are in the fifth grade, they should have "ditched the finger" and stopped pointing to each word. This practice actually retards fluency. The other strategies all enhance speed and fluency: by having them do repeated readings (answer b), they will be able to experience what fluency "feels" like; by helping readers to recognize words more quickly, they increase automaticity (answer c); and by having students read daily and use books at their independent level (answer d), they can only get better at reading and fluency.

## Question 8

The answer is *a) preconceived.* It is the only word out of the choices that contains a prefix (pre) and a root (conceive). Structural analysis deals with these components.

## Question 9

The answer is *d) class spelling tests.* Research has found these to be the least effective strategy of those listed, because many students may pass the tests yet not generalize to their own writing. The other methods support both authentic practice and ways in which to build independence in spelling.

## Question 10

The answer is *c) phonetic.* This sample has the sound features of some spellings of words, but not all—particularly vowel combinations. It has only some standard spelling, so it cannot be considered transitional. Writing in the pre-phonetic stage may have random letters, and semi-phonetic writing is only beginning to match letters with sounds. This is an example of the stage just before transitional.

# Developing Reading Comprehension and Promoting Independent Reading

# Domain III
# Third Grade Class

This third grade class is in a middle-class neighborhood. The student-to-teacher ratio is 20:1. Half of the class is African American; the other half is Caucasian. There is a high level of parent involvement—parents volunteer in the class, raise money for materials and additional services such as a full-time librarian, read to their children at home, and so on. Students have a high level of oral language and vocabulary. They also have good sight vocabulary and strong decoding skills, due to a systematic phonics program in the first grade. However, the teacher notes that many students put words in sentences that don't make sense, and they rarely self-correct. They also have difficulty answering inferential questions, and supporting and expanding their answers. Given this information and the following dialogue, decide what instructional strategies you would use before, during, and after students read.

## Dialogue 1

**TEACHER**

(having heard one student read aloud): Hmm. I'm confused by something you just read, Paul. You said, "All of a sudden a *house* came galloping down the street." I have a certain picture in my mind when you read this sentence, but it's a very strange sight. Does that make sense in this story?

**PAUL**

Oh, yeah. I meant to say "horse."

**TEACHER**

That makes more sense. Lots of people make mistakes like this one. Can you tell why people might make a mistake like this?

**PAUL**

Probably because I only looked at the letters; I didn't think about whether it made sense or not.

**TEACHER**

The letters in the words "house" and "horse" are very similar. (teacher demonstrates on the board) There are only two letters that are different. Sounding out words is a good strategy to use, but you need to ask yourself whether the words make sense in the sentence or the story.

**Dialogue 2**
(This lesson is based on the story *Molly's Pilgrim*, by Barbara Cohen, which is about a young girl who has emigrated from Russia to a small Pennsylvania town, where she is treated poorly by the other students.)

### KIM
You asked why Molly's classmates treated her so badly. I'm stuck! I can't find the answer to this question in the book. How can I find the answer?

### TEACHER
You need to find some clues in the story to get the answer. See if you can find some examples in the story of how they felt about Molly, and then guess why they would treat her the way they did.

## Brainstorming Response Ideas

### Strengths
- Consistent use of graphophonemic cue system
- Good sight vocabulary
- Good oral language and vocabulary
- Parent involvement

### Needs
- Explicit instruction for comprehension at all levels—literal, inferential and critical thinking
- Direct instruction for monitoring comprehension during reading
- Use of various methods for monitoring student progress

### Strategies
- Before or into reading: activate background knowledge, make predictions, direct instruction in questioning techniques.
- During or throughout reading: model answers to questions, especially inferential and open-ended; use direct instruction for finding support in text; use journals to ask questions, make comments, and jot down vocabulary while reading; use semantic and syntactic cues for monitoring comprehension; generate story frames and other graphic organizers; use Question, Answer, Response (QAR).
- After or beyond reading: generate story frames and other graphic organizers, using a variety of genres; model reading by using think-alouds; ask high-level or open-ended questions to stimulate "grand conversations" and higher level thinking in order to increase interaction with the text; Readers' Theatre, puppet shows, art projects, and book response journals; use Question, Answer, Response (QAR).
- Monitor progress; by choosing materials that are appropriate to student reading level; base reading level on observations; implement individual reading inventories with analyses (running records or miscues with retelling); gather student input via interest inventories and conferences.

■ For continued parent involvement, send home book bags, encourage parents to listen to retellings, conduct parent education seminars with respect to building comprehension.

## Narrative

This class needs direct instruction for comprehension at all levels—literal, inferential, and critical thinking—and they need to monitor comprehension during reading and answer questions after reading. The following strategies should be taught before, during, and after reading.

Before reading, teachers should activate the background knowledge of students by using graphic organizers or making predictions based on pictures or title. If students do not have the background knowledge for the material, teachers should provide further background information. Teachers may also model previewing the vocabulary and making predictions.

During reading, teachers should provide direct instruction in questioning techniques, such as different kinds of questions, what the questions are asking, and how to answer different questions (Question, Answer, Response, or QAR); model answers to questions on all levels; and have students find support in the text for their answer. Students should be taught to use semantic and syntactic cues for monitoring comprehension. While reading, students should ask questions, make comments, make personal connections, and jot down unknown vocabulary.

After reading, teachers and students can generate story frames and other graphic organizers, using a variety of genres. Teachers can model good reader strategies by using think-alouds; model asking open-ended questions to stimulate "grand conversations" and increase interaction with the text; and have students produce related art and drama projects, and book response journals.

# Domain III
# Eighth Grade Group

"I have just talked to the parents at back-to-school night. I teach a core class that includes English and Social Studies. A group of parents voiced their concerns that their children could read the words in their textbooks, yet they didn't understand what they were reading. They said that the kids had a hard time with homework that involved answering questions from their textbooks or looking up information in reference books and on the Internet. Further, they said that their kids don't do their homework without lots of prodding; the parents say it's a battle every night. The kids say homework is boring. I'm seeing the same thing. These particular six eighth graders (four boys, two girls) are giving me gray hair. They have excellent word attack skills and can read fluently, but they have trouble with main ideas, analyzing text, and taking notes in their learning logs."

Describe two main categories of reading and study skill strategies that this group needs for expository text. Give a rationale for your choices. Comment on what the teacher might do in response to the students' negative attitude about homework.

Make some notes of your own before turning the page.

**Strengths**

_____

_____

_____

_____

**Needs**

_____

_____

_____

_____

**Strategies**

_____

_____

_____

_____

# Brainstorming Response Ideas

## Strengths
▪ Ability to decode text and read fluently
▪ Interested parents

## Needs
▪ Strategies for comprehending expository text
▪ Reference skills and study skills
▪ Research on the Internet
▪ Inner motivation for doing homework
▪ Increased self-esteem from some success around reading/homework
▪ Ability to differentiate purposes for reading different materials

## Strategies
▪ Reading strategies—use KWL (Know, Want to Know, Learned; Ogle, 1992) SQ3R (Survey, Question, Read, Recite, Review; Robinson, 1941), or similar techniques to:
  ▪ Activate background knowledge of subject matter.
  ▪ Preview text and vocabulary.
  ▪ Make predictions.
  ▪ Ask questions.
  ▪ Set purposes for reading.
  ▪ Adjust rate to material, such as reading carefully, skimming, and scanning.
  ▪ Use learning logs and graphic organizers to record any of the pre-reading strategies listed previously.
▪ Study skills strategies—give direct instruction and model the following:
  ▪ Structure of text (location of and criteria for main idea; patterns in paragraphs, such as simple list, time-order, compare/contrast, cause/effect, problem/solution; signal words; headings and subheadings; visuals, charts, and graphs)
  ▪ Report writing (use of reference materials, Internet research, concept and vocabulary cards, outlining, note taking)
  ▪ Memory strategies
  ▪ Test taking methods
  ▪ Using learning logs and graphic organizers to record and organize new learning
▪ After or beyond reading strategies: give direct instruction and model the following:
  ▪ Using learning logs and graphic organizers to summarize and reflect on learning
  ▪ Using performance assessments, such as problem-solving projects
  ▪ Vary homework assignments in type and length and allow students some choice in homework responses (some may choose to make a graphic organizer, others may want to respond in a paragraph, etc.)

## Rationale

- Giving specific strategies for each aspect of studying text allows students to have more control over their own learning.
- Direct instruction and modeling of strategies allows students to learn the processes for studying that they can take with them and use throughout their school careers and beyond.
- Allowing variations in responses to homework assignments may lessen resistance to homework.

# Narrative

The students in this group need two different categories of strategies for expository text: reading comprehension strategies and study skills. Comprehension strategies involve such techniques as KWL or SQ3R in order to activate background knowledge of subject matter, preview text and vocabulary, make predictions, ask questions, set purposes for reading, and adjust reading rate to the type of material. Students need to use learning logs and graphic organizers to record previous learning, as well as record, organize, reflect on, and summarize new learning. Direct instruction and modeling of strategies allows students to learn the processes for studying that they can take with them and use throughout their school careers and beyond.

Students need direct instruction and modeling of reference and study skills, such as structure of expository text (location of and criteria for main idea, patterns in paragraphs, such as description, time-order, compare/contrast, cause/effect, problem/solution; signal words; headings and subheadings, etc.) and report writing (use of reference materials and skills, including the Internet, vocabulary and concept cards, outlining, and note taking).

There should be some variation in types and length of homework to allow students some choice and lessen resistance. Direct instruction and modeling of strategies gives students more control over their own learning.

# Domain III
# Sixth Grade Class

In this sixth grade class of thirty-two students, composed mostly of English speakers at various levels of abilities and skills, the teacher needs to devise strategies to deal with some issues in the comprehension of literature. Most students do not have a lot of difficulty with word attack, but their reading comprehension scores on a standardized test range from the 22nd percentile to the 65th percentile. The class engages in lively discussions around readings, but because they don't always understand the story, they have a hard time supporting their answers from the text. Given this information, along with the following summaries (based on John Steinbeck's *The Pearl*), describe two strategies that this class needs and why you would use them.

Make some notes of your own before turning the page.

**Strengths**

_____

_____

_____

_____

**Needs**

_____

_____

_____

_____

**Strategies**

_____

_____

_____

_____

## Teacher Summary

The story takes place in a poor village in the tropics where Kino, the main character, lives with his wife and baby. In this first chapter, a scorpion bites the baby, but because he thinks the family cannot pay, the doctor at first refuses to come to help. Little does he know that Kino has just found a valuable pearl on a diving expedition.

### Summary 1

Keenan lives in a small town. He got a bug bite and brought out the pearls.

### Summary 2

There were some poor people that lived in a village. One day there baby was stung by a scorpean every one came to look. the mother tryed to suck out the poisen but it didn't work that well so she said get the doctor but everyone knew the doctor would not come to them the doctor would only help the rich people so everyone in the village followed the mother and father to the doctors. He asked them if the had any money she pulled out a paper folder many times filled with 7 purals the doctor regected the 7 almost wourther (worthless) purals and said he had more immportant things to attend to.

## Summary 3

Their was this boy who had filings [feelings] bad and good and bad people were in it. It was like a dream. The boys name is Kinow. The dream was about this person who came and they were trying to do something to Kinow but Kinow wouldent let it happen.

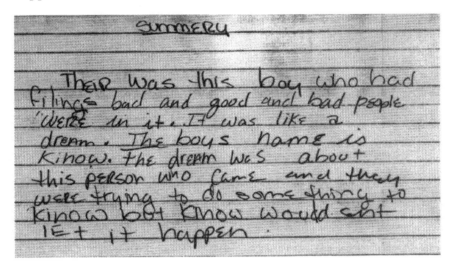

## Summary 4

The story sounds like Keno and his family are on a island. Keno is nature of the land or something like that. Keno is like a semarton [Samaritan] he always puts others needes infront of him self. When He was out side a scorpean came and stung the baby and the baby has a chance to die because of the poison. Keno and others knew about the scorpin and didn't anything about it. If they did this would have never happened.

# Brainstorming Response Ideas

## Strengths
- Word attack and word recognition skills
- Oral language—ability to take an active part in oral discussions

## Needs
- To be able to self-monitor or determine when reading is not making sense (Brown, 1980)
- To be able to synthesize and summarize main points of what has been read and/or discussed
- To be able to support ideas with references to specific parts of text

## Strategies and Rationale
- Before reading, use think-aloud strategy to show students how good readers monitor their own reading (Nist & Kirby, 1986; Randall, Fairbanks & Kennedy, 1986):
  - Read part of chapter or story aloud.
  - Make predictions as you read; confirm or correct your predictions.
  - Reread when text does not make sense.
  - Note parts that show major element of story—characters, plot, setting, major action (on the board, overhead, or chart paper).
  - Ask questions of yourself about parts of the text.
  - Point out parts of the text that support your understanding.
- During reading, have students make predictions and take notes in their learning log or mark the places in the story or chapter where the reading does not make sense to them; doing this begins to get students in the habit of monitoring their comprehension while they read.
- After reading:
  - Discuss and practice using criteria for a main idea (not too broad, not a detail, not outside the topic); have students practice giving titles to short paragraphs.
  - Guide students in the use of graphic organizers (Venn diagrams, webs, or clusters), outlines, or notes to help them identify main points.
- Provide direct instruction and model writing summaries from graphic organizers so that students have a better understanding of the process of summary writing as well as what a summary actually looks like.
- Use the think-aloud instructional strategy to model how good readers interact with the text by activating background knowledge, clarifying ideas in the text, locating main events/ideas, asking questions, and summarizing.
- Model how to take notes, and mark where the story was confusing.
- Have students take part in Literature Circles (small groups reading the same material; can be integrated with buddy or partner reading; discuss story in small group). Literature Circles build confidence in discussion skills because students have an opportunity to rehearse discussion in a small group setting, which will then generalize to the larger group.

## Narrative

One of the major needs of this group is to be able to self-monitor or determine when reading is not making sense. The teacher can use the think-aloud strategy to show students how good readers monitor their own reading. The teacher should demonstrate that good readers make predictions as they read; they confirm or correct their predictions; they reread when text doesn't make sense; they note parts that show major elements of story (characters, plot, setting, major action); they ask questions; they clarify ideas; and they locate parts of the text that support their understanding. The think-aloud method allows the teacher to model all of these strategies that good readers use.

Once the teacher has modeled this method, students can practice in pairs by thinking aloud with each other. As they interact with the text, they can make predictions, take notes in their learning logs, or mark the places in the story or chapter where the reading does not make sense to them. Doing this begins to get students in the habit of monitoring while they read. After they have tried the think-aloud, students can list the strategies that they used while reading together. They share their lists with the rest of the class.

Another major need of this group is summary writing. After discussion, have students practice using the criteria for main events, and guide students in the use of graphic organizers to identify main events in the story and make the distinction between minor events and major events. Model writing summaries from graphic organizers so that students have a better understanding of the process of summary writing as well as what a summary actually looks like. The use of upper-level picture books works well for the introduction of this process.

# Multiple-Choice Questions

## Question 1
Mrs. Lemon does a read-aloud/think-aloud several times a week in her first grade classroom. Which of the following strategies is she *not* modeling?
   a) phonetic analysis
   b) making connections with the text
   c) asking questions of the text, author, and self
   d) checking predictions

## Question 2
Juan, Samir, Suzie, and Pat are in Mr. Edward's fourth grade, and have difficulty with summarizing what they've read. Which of the following strategies would *not* be an effective solution for this problem?
   a) using a graphic organizer
   b) using reciprocal teaching
   c) modeling the summarizing process
   d) using the cloze procedure

## Question 3
Mr. Edwards also has several students in his fourth grade class who need more strategies for comprehension of text. Which of the following strategies would *not* be effective for these students?
   a) looking up vocabulary words during reading
   b) activating prior knowledge before reading
   c) using context clues for monitoring
   d) checking and modifying predictions while reading

## Question 4
Which pair of similar instructional strategies could Mr. Edwards best use for improving comprehension?
   a) KWL and buddy reading
   b) QAR and SQ3R
   c) graphic organizers and think-alouds
   d) reciprocal teaching and Literature Circles

## Question 5
Ms. Redcloud gave an assessment of literary elements to her sixth grade class. Which of the following would be included on her list of elements?
   a) setting and time
   b) character
   c) theme or moral
   d) all of the above

### Question 6

In her book discussions, Ms. Redcloud uses various levels of comprehension questions. First, she introduces the different types of questions. Next, she models different types of questions using fairy tales. Finally, students make up their own questions in the different categories. Ms. Redcloud's student Jose gave this question for discussion: "How does Cinderella show that life is like a wheel—sometimes you are on top and sometimes you're on the bottom?" What type of question is this an example of?

 a) inference
 b) literal
 c) main idea
 d) critical thinking

### Question 7

Mrs. Malula has an eighth grade social studies class. They need note-taking, outlining, and study skills. Which strategy should she begin to model, teach, and have students practice first?

 a) patterns of expository text
 b) reciprocal teaching
 c) sequencing
 d) main idea

### Question 8

Mr. Lutz recognizes the importance of supporting at-home reading for his third graders. Which of the following would *not* promote this program?

 a) During back-to-school night, model reading strategies for parents to use with their children.
 b) Send book bags home as part of regular homework.
 c) Have parental partnership to "turn off the TV."
 d) Use an Author's Chair.

# Answers to Multiple-Choice Questions

### Question 1

The answer is *a) phonetic analysis.* Mrs. Lemon is not modeling phonetic analysis, because she is an expert reader and has achieved fluency and thus automaticity in terms of phonetic analysis. During read alouds/think alouds, Mrs. Lemon is demonstrating how an expert reader interacts with text during reading. Answers b, c, and d are all examples of how a good reader interacts with text.

## Question 2

The answer is *d) using the cloze procedure*. The cloze procedure is an instructional tool for teaching students how to use context clues. Answers a, b, and c are effective strategies for teaching students who are having difficulty with summarizing; graphic organizers could be part of modeling the process of summarizing, and reciprocal teaching provides good practice for summarizing.

## Question 3

The answer is *a) looking up vocabulary words during reading*, which is too time consuming and will interrupt the meaning-making process as a whole. Teaching the student to use context clues contributes to the meaning-making process, and is more efficient and effective. Answers b and d allow readers to get ready to read the text and to monitor what they are reading.

## Question 4

The answer is *d) reciprocal teaching and literature circles*; these strategies are similar. In each one, small groups of students assume the role of the teacher and discuss the text in depth by asking questions, summarizing, making predictions, and clarifying the text. KWL and buddy reading (answer a) are not alike, because the first deals with activating background knowledge and adding to that knowledge and the second involves reading with a partner. Questioning the author (QAR) and SQ3R (answer b) are not similar, because the first is a form of questioning and the second is a study strategy. Graphic organizers and think-alouds (answer c) are not alike, because one is a technique for visually organizing ideas, and the other is a method of modeling what good readers do.

## Question 5

The answer is *d) all of the above*. Answers a, b, and c are all literary elements and each should be part of the instruction and discussion of good literature.

## Question 6

The answer is *d) critical thinking*. Critical-thinking questions require the reader to evaluate and use background knowledge to answer. Inference (answer a) would involve putting together clues embedded in the story along with background knowledge. A literal question (answer b) would be directly stated in the story. A main idea (answer c) would require the reader to choose the event that was most important to the story.

## Question 7

The answer is *d) main idea*. Being able to determine the main idea is the basic component of note taking, outlining, and effective studying. Examining patterns of expository text (answer a) is important after students can tell the difference between relevant and irrelevant information in text. Reciprocal teaching (answer b) is an instructional tool to facilitate students' interaction with the text. Graphic organizers (answer c) would be useful in understanding expository text, but students still need to be able to identify the main idea before they can organize the information visually.

## Question 8

The answer is *d) use an Author's Chair*. The Author's Chair is a component of a writer's workshop. During this time, students share their writing with the class. Answers a, b, and c all promote at-home reading.

# IV

# Supporting Reading Through Oral and Written Language Development

# Domain IV
# Second Grade Group

Mrs. Roberts has twenty students in her second grade class, all from a suburban neighborhood. It is the beginning of the year and students are at various stages of literacy from the emergent to the independent stage. All the students are motivated to read, regardless of their reading level. They enjoy books and going to the library. The teacher is concerned about a small group of emergent readers who need to enhance their skills. Although they have basic skills in phonics, she notices that they are still reading word by word without expression, and they are even attempting to decode sight words. Because they are still using their fingers to track across the lines of text, their reading is slow and laborious. What are this group's strengths and needs, and what three techniques would you have Mrs. Roberts use to address these problems? Tell why you would use each technique.

Make some notes of your own before turning the page.

**Strengths**

_____
_____
_____
_____
_____

**Needs**

_____
_____
_____
_____
_____

**Techniques**

_____
_____
_____
_____
_____

# Brainstorming Response Ideas

## Strengths
- Some understanding of phonics skills
- Motivated to read; enjoy books

## Needs
- Increased fluency
- Use of expression

## Techniques
- To increase fluency, use choral reading that will:
    - Allow students to practice reading in phrases rather than word by word.
    - Help students recognize the role of punctuation in aiding expression and enhancing meaning.
- Use repeated readings of familiar texts.
- Use buddy reading or partner reading to practice in a smaller setting.
- Encourage students to use a tape recorder to listen to their own reading.
- Increase students' understanding of syntax and grammatical structure, and, at the same time, increase their ability to make connections between oral or spoken language and written text structures.
- Use Readers' Theatre (students rewrite a book or a story in play form) and have students present the finished product to an audience, which will enhance reading fluency and oral language and is motivating for students.

# Narrative

Although they have an understanding of basic phonics skills, this group needs to increase fluency and expression. To increase fluency, Mrs. Roberts might use three techniques. The first technique she could use is choral reading, to allow students to practice reading fluently and to read in phrases instead of single words. The second technique involves repeated readings of familiar texts, either via buddy reading (partner reading) or having students use tape recorders to read along with stories and to listen to themselves read, which allows them to practice the same story to the point of fluency. The third technique to promote fluency and expression in her students' reading is the use of Readers' Theatre. Students practice fluency using creative expression, with a text that they have translated into play form. This technique allows practice in a fun, motivating way.

# Domain IV
# Sixth Grade Class

This inner-city seventh grade class has thirty-five students, many of whom are Hispanic second-generation Americans. Although they generally have English-language decoding skills and can understand the main points of the stories they read, they have difficulty with some other aspects of the text. Read the following excerpts from class discussions on the book *Bridge to Terabithia* by Katherine Paterson. After every discussion, determine what strategies the teacher has initiated and what instructional step she would/should take next.

## Discussion 1

**TEACHER**
Why was Jess reluctant to go to Terabithia without Leslie?

**STUDENTS**
(no immediate response)

**TEACHER**
What do you think "reluctant" means?

**STUDENT 1**
Felt funny about it?

**TEACHER**
Tell me more about that.

**STUDENT 1**
I'm not sure. I really didn't understand that.

**TEACHER**
Do you think he wanted to go to Terabithia by himself?

**STUDENT 2**
No.

**TEACHER**
What makes you think so? Go back and read those lines at the bottom of page 65, and see if you can tell what it means using the author's words.

## Discussion 2

**TEACHER**
What words did you write down in your journal that gave you trouble, that you didn't know?

**STUDENT 1**
I didn't know what "suppress" means.

**TEACHER**
So, what strategy could you use when you run into a word you don't know?

**STUDENT 1**
Look it up in the dictionary.

**TEACHER**
How else could you find out what it means?

**STUDENT 1**
Ask the teacher.

**TEACHER**
We'll have to work on some other ways. Let me give you another sentence using the word "suppress": "I couldn't *suppress* my anger when the big guy punched me in the nose." Given this hint, talk to your partner and see if you can decide what "suppress" means.

## Discussion 3

**TEACHER**
Does anyone else have another word they wrote down?

**STUDENT 2**
What does "a-b-s-o-r-b-e-d" mean? How do you say it?

**TEACHER**
(Pronounces "absorbed.") Do you remember that we had that word in science when we talked about how the roots of the plant absorbed all the water in the glass?

**STUDENT 3**
But May Belle wasn't drinking any water. She was watching TV.

## Discussion 1: Instructional Emphasis

_____

_____

_____

_____

_____

_____

_____

_____

## Discussion 2: Instructional Emphasis

_____

_____

_____

_____

_____

_____

_____

_____

## Discussion 3: Instructional Emphasis

_____

_____

_____

_____

_____

_____

_____

_____

# Brainstorming Response Ideas

### Discussion 1
- Rereading the text for context clues in sections before and after the word

### Discussion 2
- Synonyms based on familiar context; discussing with a partner
- Have students substitute the synonym in the text to determine whether it makes sense in the context

### Discussion 3
- Multiple meanings, analogy
- Context clues
- Structural analysis
- Consult other sources-peers, teachers, dictionary, thesaurus, computer

# Narrative

In Discussion 1, the teacher's emphasis is on learning vocabulary through the use of context clues. Her next step should be direct instruction and modeling by showing the students how to make sense of the word "reluctant" in its original sentence; by showing the students how to read the prior text and the text that follows to find clues that will give the meaning of the word.

In Discussion 2, the teacher's instructional emphasis is on an alternative strategy, such as putting the word in a different sentence that is closer to students' experience. Then the teacher asks students to discuss the meaning of the word "suppress" in this new context. She then asks students to determine the meaning by discussing possible synonyms. Next, the teacher should provide direct instruction in making a decision about whether the synonym(s) makes sense in the original context.

In Discussion 3, the teacher's emphasis is on multiple meanings and the use of teaching through analogy. The student in the discussion understood the word "absorbed" in the expository text, but not in the narrative. The next step is for the teacher to give direct instruction in the different meanings within the context of the narrative and the expository text. The following step might be to use structural analysis—including word origins, roots, suffixes, and prefixes—to further clarify the meaning of the word. The word "absorbed" lends itself to both the use of context clues and word study. The teacher should advise the students to consult another source—ask a peer, a teacher, or another reference (computer, thesaurus, or dictionary)—but she must model and have students practice the efficient use of sources.

# Domain IV
# Fifth Grade Individual

Byron is a fifth grader who is considered to be "cool" by his classmates. He is at the independent reading stage; however, Byron does not choose to do any reading on his own for enjoyment. According to Byron, reading is not cool. He balks at going to the library, and disrupts the class during Silent Sustained Reading. Name four methods you would use to help Byron and other reluctant readers be more engaged in good literature and reading in general.

Make some notes of your own before turning the page.

**Strengths**

_____

_____

_____

_____

_____

_____

**Needs**

_____

_____

_____

_____

_____

_____

**Strategies**

_____

_____

_____

_____

_____

# Brainstorming Response Ideas

### Strengths
- Is able to read independently
- Has social skills

### Needs
- More exposure to quality literature
- Better connections to different literary genres
- Motivation to read independently

### Strategies
- Hold individual conference for interest inventory.
- Provide many diverse types of reading materials.
- Display books and reading corner attractively.
- Read aloud thought-provoking literature.

## Narrative

First, hold an individual conference with Byron to determine his interests beyond the world of the classroom, and help Byron find books along his lines of interest. For independent reading, provide many diverse types of reading materials that span different reading levels, cultures, and genres, such as mystery, sports fantasy, biography and autobiography, etc., providing him with lots of choices. Display books attractively, have comfortable chairs and pillows, and have a reading corner. Do "book talks" to stimulate interest in particular books (briefly discuss the characters, plot, and setting, and stop when something interesting is about to happen); have students also do book talks, which can often encourage others to read the book. Finally, read aloud to the class using thought-provoking literature that has personal connections to the age group and the interests of the class.

# Multiple-Choice Questions

## Question 1
Mrs. Kalua has a class of fifth graders, half of whom are second language learners. Which of the following is probably the most difficult for the English language learners?

a) oral language development
b) LEA
c) multiple meanings
d) idioms

## Question 2
In her daily instructional plans to support English language learners with scaffolding strategies, which of the following would Mrs. Kalua be most likely to use?

a) realia (objects/artifacts)
b) graphic organizers
c) double entry journals
d) a and b

## Question 3
Mrs. Kalua needs to make decisions about her instructional plan for vocabulary development. Which of the following would *not* contribute to vocabulary development?

a) cloze procedure
b) semantic mapping
c) read-alouds
d) sight words

## Question 4
Mrs. Dempsey has a new second grade class, half of whom are second language learners in different stages of English language development. Which of the following methods would be most effective in determining strengths and needs in oral language development?

a) journal writing samples
b) observations and developmental checklists
c) reading comprehension questions
d) San Diego Quick

## Question 5
Mrs. Dempsey also needs to assess her students' writing. Which of the following methods would be most effective in determining strengths and needs in written language development?

a) spelling test
b) informal reading inventory
c) writing samples
d) workbook pages

# Answers to Multiple-Choice Questions

## Question 1

The answer is *d) idioms*, because they are outside of the English language learner's cultural experience. Idioms are also difficult because even though the words may be simple, they do not convey their everyday dictionary meaning. Answer c, multiple meanings, is a close second, but the context of a sentence can help with those, and one of the meanings is generally found in the dictionary. Development of English language syntax (grammatical structure) and language experience approach (LEA) are both helpful to English language learners.

## Question 2

The answer is *d) a and b*. Realia (objects/artifacts) create concrete connections to new words and add tactile and kinesthetic dimensions to learning. Graphic organizers provide support for students having difficulty with the comprehension of text by having them organize the information pictorially. Double entry journals (answer c), though helpful for readers and writers of English, might not be helpful for the various stages of English language learning.

## Question 3

The answer is *d) sight words*. Although very useful in allowing readers to gain fluency, sight words alone do not expand meaningful vocabulary. Oral language development through read-alouds, the cloze procedure, and semantic mapping help to increase word understanding.

## Question 4

The answer is *b) observations and developmental checklists*, through which a teacher can monitor the different phases and elements of oral language development. Given these choices, listening to a student speak in formal and informal situations is the best way to evaluate English language development. Journal writing samples (answer a) deal with written language; reading comprehension questions (answer c) deal with reading; and the San Diego Quick (answer d) deals with knowledge of words read in isolation.

## Question 5

The answer is *c) writing samples*. Writing samples show how the student is able to apply spelling rules, grammar, and other facets of writing in an authentic context. A spelling test (answer a) shows only a student's ability to memorize words, and workbook pages (answer d) do not show the student's ability to apply the pattern presented in daily writing situations.

# DOMAINS

# I–IV

# Domains I–IV
## First Grade Individual

Frank is a first grader who will turn six in November. English is Frank's first language. He comes from a middle-class family, with two parents who read to him on a regular basis. He actively participates in class discussions, even though there are times when he will make an error in syntax with verb forms, like "runned" for "run."

At independent reading time, Frank chooses picture books and pores over the pictures, but does not spend much time focusing on the words. If he does choose a book with more words, it is usually a book about sharks or dinosaurs. Given this information and the following assessments, explain where Frank is in his literacy development, give four of his major strengths, and—based on his needs—describe in depth three instructional strategies that you would recommend for him and why.

**Checklist for Observing Concepts about Print**

NAME

Frank S.

| | | | | | | | | | | | | |
|---|---|---|---|---|---|---|---|---|---|---|---|---|
| Time at school | K | | | | | | | | | | | |
| Front of book | ✓ | | | | | | | | | | | |
| Print contains message | ✓ | | | | | | | | | | | |
| Where to start | ✓ | | | | | | | | | | | |
| Left to right | ✓ | | | | | | | | | | | |
| Return sweep | ✓ | | | | | | | | | | | |
| Word by word matching | ✓ | | | | | | | | | | | |
| First and last | ✓ | | | | | | | | | | | |
| Print is right way up | ✓ | | | | | | | | | | | |
| Left page before right | ✓ | | | | | | | | | | | |
| Full stop | — | | | | | | | | | | | |
| Question mark | ✓ | | | | | | | | | | | |
| Capital and lower case letter correspondence | ✓ | | | | | | | | | | | |
| Letters | ✓ | | | | | | | | | | | |
|   Recognizes difference/ knows the term. | | | | | | | | | | | | |
| Words | ✓ | | | | | | | | | | | |
| First and last letters of words | ✓ | | | | | | | | | | | |
| Capital letters | ✓ | | | | | | | | | | | |
| Comments | | | | | | | | | | | | |

This page is copyright-free

**Legend**

✓ knows
0 does not know
— does not know
0✓ corrected by student

*Table 5.1* **Alphabet Recognition Test**   Frank S.

A✓ S✓ D✓ F✓ G✓ H✓ J✓

K✓ L✓ P✓ O✓ I✓ U✓ Y✓

T✓ R✓ E✓ W✓ Q✓ Z✓(x sc) X✓

C✓ V✓ B✓ N✓ M✓

a✓ s✓ (d)b✓ f✓ g✓ h✓ (j)i

k✓ l✓(i sc) p✓ o✓ i✓ u✓ y✓

t✓ r✓ e✓ w✓ q P z✓(x sc) x✓

c✓ v✓ b✓ n✓ m✓ a✓ y✓

g✓ q P t✓ a✓ g✓ t✓ q P

From Margaret Ann Richek, et al. *Reading Problems: Assessment and Teaching Strategies*
(Third Edition). Needham, Massachusetts: Allyn and Bacon, 1996

*Table 5.2* **Assessing Phonological Awareness: Blending and Segmenting**

*Directions:* I am going to say some words in a special code and I want you to figure out the real word. If I say s/-/a/-/t/, you say *sat*. If I say /p/-/i/-/g/, you say *pig*.

| Teacher says: | Expected Response | Student's Response |
|---|---|---|
| /d/-/i/-/g/ | dig | dig |
| /p/-/u/-/l/ | pull | pull |
| /b/-/e/-/d/ | bed | bed |
| /f/-/a/-/s/-/t/ | fast | fast |
| /s/-/o/-/f/-/t/ | soft | soft |

*Directions:* Now we will change jobs. If I say *bat*, you say /b/-/a/-/t/. If I say *feet*, you say /f/-/ee/-/t/.

| Teacher says: | Expected Response | Student's Response |
|---|---|---|
| can | /c/-/a/-/n/ | c / a / n |
| tell | /t/-/e/-/l/ | t / e / l l |
| dust | /d/-/u/-/s/-/t/ | d / u / s / t |
| sit | /s/-/i/-/t/ | s / i / t |
| fog | /f/-/o/-/g/ | f / o / g |

NOTE: When a letter is enclosed in brackets (//), this indicates that you should say the letter *sound*.

Frank S.

*Table 5.3* **Assessing Letter–Sound Correspondences: Beginning Letter Sounds**

*Practice:* What is the beginning sound of *mat*? (Student should say /m/.) What letter makes that sound? (Student should say "M." If not, model and practice another word.)

| Word | Beginning Sound | Beginning Letter |
|---|---|---|
| fish | /f/ | f |
| little | /l/ | l |
| ride | /r/ | r |
| want | /w/ | u |
| happy | /h/ | h |

From Margaret Ann Richek, et al. *Reading Problems: Assessment and Teaching Strategies* (Third Edition). Needham, Massachusetts: Allyn and Bacon, 1996

# The Box and the Fox

The old fox saw a box.
*(dk dk   dk dk marked above: old, fox, saw, a)*

He said, "What is this?"

The box said, "I am a box."

The fox said, "What is a box?"

The box said, "A box is a box.  What are you?"

The fox said, "I am a fox."

The box said, "What is a fox?"

The fox said, "A fox is a fox."

So, a box is a box and a fox is a fox.

Frank S. — very slow word-by-word, but read whole story with help.

___ = did not know

**Graded Reading Passages Test: Form B—Narrative** *Frank S.* *Listening*

### A Snowy Day (1)

**COMPREHENSION CHECK**

INTRODUCTION: Please read this story to find out what two children like to do.

*A Snowy Day*

Bill and Kim looked out the window. They were very happy. It was snowing. They wanted to go out to play.

Bill and Kim could not wait to build something with the snow. When they went outside, they made two large balls. They put one on top of the other. Then they made one small ball. They put it on the very top. Then Bill and Kim used some sticks and stones. Now they were done.

**Accountable Miscues**

Full Miscues: _____ × 1 = _____

Half Miscues: _____ × ½ = _____

TOTAL _____

| | Probed Recall | Free Recall |
|---|---|---|
| L 1. What were the names of the two children in the story? (Bill and Kim) | _____ | ✓ |
| L 2. Why were Bill and Kim very happy? (They saw it was snowing.) | _____ | ✓ |
| L 3. How many balls of snow did Bill and Kim make? (3) | _____ | ✓ |
| L 4. Where did they put the small ball? (on the top) | _____ | ✓ |
| I 5. What do you think Bill and Kim built with the white flakes? (a snowman) | _____ | ✓ |
| C 6. Could this story have happened? What makes you think so? (Accept any logical response, such as "Because the events sound real.") | _____ | ✓ |

*Yes, because people really do build snowmen.*

Total Comprehension Errors  **0**  (L & I)

<u>Retell</u> The boys wanted to play in the snow. They were using sticks and stones to make a snowman.

From Ezra L. Stieglitz. *The Stieglitz Informal Reading Inventory.* (Second Edition) Boston, Massachusetts: Allyn and Bacon 1997

I bI 200PR 20C R 2
ot to Ys. Rue.

FRank

I buy Super Soakers at Toys-R-US.

Make some notes of your own before turning the page.

## Strengths

_____

_____

_____

_____

_____

_____

_____

_____

## Needs

_____

_____

_____

_____

_____

_____

_____

_____

## Strategies and Rationale

_____

_____

_____

_____

_____

_____

_____

_____

## Brainstorming Response Ideas

### Strengths
- Literacy development is age-appropriate
- Read to by parents and teacher
- Actively participates in class discussions
- Phonemic awareness—can segment and blend whole words
- Can identify most letters with their corresponding sounds
- Sight word vocabulary in early stages
- Can read short sentences using predictable text
- Listening comprehension; is able to retell story in sequence
- Stays on task during independent reading
- Attempts invented spelling—uses beginning and ending consonants and some vowels
- Can write a complete sentence
- Has some idea of word spacing, capital letters, and periods

### Needs
- Development time
- Some continuing problems around verb forms (syntax) in oral language
- Some continuing problems with reversals in letter identification in reading and writing
- Some difficulty with initial consonant sounds, as in w, h, c, k
- Sight vocabulary
- Fluency
- Focus on words in independent reading
- Spelling (encoding) medial sounds, particularly vowels
- Increased pencil control (fine motor control)

### Strategies and Rationale
- Implement vocabulary extension and modeling of verb forms through read-alouds and oral language (most children outgrow this with time)
- Increase sight vocabulary through immersion in environmental print, such as word walls, reading the room, sight word games, practice reading words in poems and chants (choral reading), keeping word book/dictionary, reading predictable books in shared reading and independent reading, practice using kinesthetic/tactile techniques (tracing, sandpaper letters).
- For increased word attack skills (decoding), make or use commercial word games with onsets and rimes, rhyming words, word families, read decodable text, practice with sound blending, practice with counting syllables (clapping, snapping fingers).
- For increased comprehension:
    - Before reading (into): Use pre-reading strategies, such as: activate background knowledge about subject, guide student through a picture walk, have him make predictions using title and pictures, and pre-teach new or difficult vocabulary.

- During reading (through): Ask questions during shared reading for checking understanding and checking predictions, use oral cloze to encourage use of context clues (syntactic and semantic cue system), along with graphophonemic cues to self-monitor or cross-check for meaning (ask: Does that word make sense? Does it look like the word in the story?).
- After reading (beyond): Ask high level, open-ended questions to increase student's interaction with text and encourage more in-depth discussion, use extension activities such as reader's theatre, simple semantic maps/webs, reading response journal, acting out the story, puppet theater, drawings showing main events in beginning, middle and end to promote awareness of sequence.

- For fluency, use repeated readings with choral reading, echo reading, buddy reading; tape record student's reading; and promote independent reading.
- For writing, give opportunities to generate text every day using word walls, personal and commercial dictionaries, word stretching games to increase ability to distinguish medial and ending sounds, interactive (shared) writing, spelling program around word patterns (*cvc* and so on), oral spelling games using individual chalkboards, making words, and so on.
- Introduce language experience stories (reading back his own dictated text).
- For writing between the lines, use modeling, interactive writing, and practice on slate boards and paper (fine motor skills will improve with time).
- Use direct instruction in reversals in reading and writing to encourage self-monitoring.

## Narrative

Frank just entered the emergent reader stage, and despite the reversals that he is still making, he is between the phonemic and transitional stages of writing. Therefore, he is developmentally on target for his age in both reading and writing. Based on several pieces of evidence, he has many strengths. Four of these strengths stand out. When read to he is able to retell details in sequence (listening comprehension), he has concepts about print, he has developed phonemic awareness, and he is starting to decode and encode using initial consonants.

Frank needs direct, systematic instruction in phonics, such as vowel sounds, onsets and rimes (blends and word patterns), segmentation, rhymes, and syllables. These skills can be taught through activities such as letter and word games, individual slate board work, centers, and so on. Word sorts would be of particular value for the learning of phonics. For example, if the teacher's instruction involves the discrimination between short vowel *a* and short vowel *e*, he/she could present the selection of words in a pocket chart, help Frank decode each word, and have him put it into the appropriate category. This type of activity could also be used as a center activity. In addition to systematic instruction in phonics, the teacher can also do instruction using embedded phonics. This method involves text, such as a language experience story, to identify phonics generalizations that occur in the text, and are extracted for study. Further, the teacher needs to help Frank apply the decoding strategies to reading poems, chants, and decodable text that contain the phonics patterns previously taught.

Secondly, Frank needs to increase his sight vocabulary. Learning sight words requires memory and a variety of activities in order to keep him involved in the learning. These various activities should include immersion in environmental print, such as word walls; reading the room; sight word games; practice reading words in poems and chants (choral reading); keeping a word book, cards, or a dictionary; reading predictable books in shared reading and independent reading; and practice using kinesthetic/tactile techniques like VAKT (tracing words, using sandpaper letters, and sand).

Third, Frank also needs instruction in comprehension strategies in order for reading to make sense to him. The instruction should take place during guided reading group time, and should include Before, During, and After strategies. The Before strategies consist of activating background knowledge, making predictions, doing picture walks, and previewing new vocabulary. The During strategies include shared reading, and choral reading, which allows students to practice both phonics and comprehension strategies. This is the place where the teacher can guide students through the reading by giving support (scaffolding). This phase can also contain oral cloze exercises to encourage the use of context clues (syntactic and semantic cues, along with graphophonemic cues), and self-monitoring strategies or cross-checking for meaning. (Ask: Does that word make sense? Does it look like the word in the story?) In the After phase, to increase Frank's interaction with text, instruction should include practice in retelling, the use of critical thinking questions, in-depth discussion, semantic maps, drama, puppets, and drawings showing sequence of main events. In order to increase fluency and independence, Frank should reread familiar stories, using both choral reading and reading with a buddy.

# Domains I–IV
# Third Grade Individual

Manuel is a third grader who speaks English but understands Tagalog and Spanish. At the beginning of the year, as part of gathering baseline information, his teacher interviewed him, gave him an informal reading inventory, and had him do a writing sample. During observations of his reading and writing behaviors in the first few days of school, the teacher noticed problems with fluency and confidence in reading. He was much more eager to do the writing sample than read. Given this information and the following data, choose one area of need in reading and one area of need in writing, and discuss three major strategies for each area of need.

## Interview

**Teacher**
Do you like to read?

**Manuel**
It depends on the book.

**Teacher**
What kinds of books do you like best?

**Manuel**
I like books with lots of pictures because chapter books are harder.

**Teacher**
What do you do when you get stuck on a word when you're reading?

**Manuel**
I do the word by parts, cut them by places, like *to/day*.

**Teacher**
What do you do if that doesn't work?

**Manuel**
I go and ask somebody to tell me.

**Teacher**
What if no one is around?

**Manuel**
I sound it out.

**Teacher**
What do you think about writing?

**Manuel**

It's good. I like it.

**Teacher**

What do you like to write?

**Manuel**

I like to make really long stories like chapters.

**Teacher**

It appears that you like writing more than reading. Why is that?

**Manuel**

Cause I'm not saying the words, I'm writing the words how I think it is.

**Scoring Sheet**                                    **3C (LI)**

B-12

Judy's class ~~was going on~~ a trip to visit an airport. *Before they left they read* some books *about* airplanes *and* airplane pilots. Everyone *in the class was* excited *when it came time to go.*

The class rode (to) the airport *in a big yellow bus.* After the bus stopped, the first person *to get off was* Judy's *teacher. She told the class that they* must *all* stay together *so that none of the students would get* lost.

First, they visited *the ticket counter and* learned *how* passengers *buy their* tickets. Then a pilot came *and told them he would take them on a large airplane.* After they were inside *the airplane everyone was* surprised *because it was so* large. When Judy's class got *back to school they all said they* wanted *to visit the* airport *again.*

---

**Retell:** *They went to a trip to the airport. They wanted to go to the airport again.*

---

**Questions:**

F 1. ____√____ Where was Judy's class going? (To visit an airport)

F 2. ____√____ What did they do before they left? (They read some books, or they read some books about airplanes and airplane pilots)

F 3. Don't know How did the class feel when it was time to go? (They were excited)

F 4. Don't know How did the class get to the airport? (They rode in a bus, or in a big yellow bus)

F 5. ____√____ Who was the first person to get off the bus? (Judy's teacher, or the teacher)

F 6. ____√____ What did the teacher tell the class when they first got off the bus? (That they must stay together, or that they must stay together so they would not get lost)

F 7. Don't know What did they visit first? (The ticket counter)

V 8. ____√____ In this story it said the students learned how the passengers buy their tickets. What is a passenger? (Someone who rides on an airplane)

F 9. ____X____ When the pilot came to meet the class what did he tell them? (He told them he would take them on an airplane, or on a large airplane)

I 10. Don't know What did the class say that would make you think they liked their visit to the airport? (They said they wanted to visit the airport again)

From Eldon E. Ekwall & James L. Shanker. *Ekwall/Shanker Reading Inventory.* (3rd Edition) Boston, MA: Allyn & Bacon, 1993

Succor

My Favoret thing to do is succor I like being dyfens my taem is the blue dyens

Make some notes of your own before turning the page.

**One Need in Reading**

_____

_____

_____

_____

_____

_____

**One Need in Writing**

_____

_____

_____

_____

_____

_____

**Strategies for Need in Reading**

_____

_____

_____

_____

_____

_____

**Strategies for Need in Writing**

_____

_____

_____

_____

_____

_____

_____

# Response Ideas

## Need in Reading

- Monitoring for meaning because he uses the graphophonemic cue system almost exclusively; most miscues result in loss of meaning

## Strategies to Address Need in Reading

- Model the use of semantic cue system through the use of context clues (reread, read on, go back and put in word that makes sense in the context).
- Ask student to practice with cloze procedure.
- Model the use of monitoring through read-aloud/think-alouds (self-correction of reading errors/miscues, ask questions about whether words make sense, such as *"What is a pilot?"*).
- Ask student to practice with monitoring strategies.
- Within guided reading group: Provide opportunities for pre-reading strategies (into), such as pre-teaching vocabulary, activating background knowledge, scaffolding.
- During (through) reading: Provide scaffolding for student when he gets stuck on a word or makes inappropriate substitutions.
- After reading (beyond): Show student how monitoring will help him retell the story with greater detail and answer questions.

## Need in Writing

- Elaboration, since he is a third grader (mechanics are secondary)

## Strategies to Address Need in Writing

- Ask student to tell story orally, encourage detail by asking questions.
- Ask student to write about what he just said.
- Model elaboration in writing using overhead.
- Select examples of expert writers that show elaboration and detail.
- Have student evaluate two pieces of writing from a former class, showing one with sparse details and one with more detail.

# Narrative

Since Manuel uses graphophonemic cues almost exclusively, which many times result in a loss of meaning, he needs strategies for monitoring so that he brings meaning to text. Some of the strategies to teach this include modeling the use of the semantic cue system through the use of context clues, rereading, reading on, and going back to put in a word that makes sense in the sentence. He needs to add this strategy to his skills in graphophonemics. Manuel can then practice with cloze procedure to use context. Another strategy the teacher can use is think-alouds to model monitoring, self-correcting, and asking questions of himself about whether words make sense, such as "What is a pilot?" Manuel would then practice this procedure in a small group or with a partner. In addition, within his guided reading group, the teacher should provide opportunities for pre-reading strategies (Into stage), such as activating background knowledge, pre-teaching vocabulary and scaffolding with a picture walk, and making predictions. The teacher can also teach monitoring strategies during reading (Through stage) by providing instruction when Manuel gets stuck on a word or makes inappropriate substitutions. After reading (Beyond stage), the teacher can show Manuel how monitoring will help him retell the story with greater detail and answer the questions.

In writing, although Manuel needs support for spelling and other mechanics such as capitalization and punctuation, his major need is for elaboration in the pieces. While in the interview he says he prefers writing over reading, and although he says he likes to make really long stories, he wrote very little for the writing sample. In order for Manuel to add detail to his writing, the teacher can ask him to tell the story orally, encouraging details by asking questions to clarify what he's saying. Then the teacher can ask him to write down what he just said. Another instructional strategy the teacher could use is to model elaboration in writing using her own text on the overhead. He/she could also show Manuel examples of expert writers who demonstrate elaboration and detail. Additionally, he/she can have Manuel compare and evaluate two pieces of writing from a former class, showing one with sparse details and one with more detail.

# Domains I–IV
# Fourth Grade Individual

Ramon is a first-semester fourth grader. Tagalog is Ramon's first language; he moved to the United States last year. Although he is fairly proficient orally in English during informal class situations and outside with his peers, his shy demeanor prevents him from participating in class discussions. When asked to evaluate his reading, Ramon said he "just reads words" and forgets what he reads. He wants to read bigger vocabulary words so that he can read Harry Potter books (chapter books). Writing samples show Ramon's problems to be in the area of grammatical structure for both words and sentences. His informal reading inventory with retelling follows. His standardized achievement test scores from the prior year show:

- Reading at 2.8 grade level (20th percentile)
- Vocabulary skills at the 2.0 grade level (6th percentile)
- Spelling skills at the 3.0 grade level (23rd percentile)
- English language usage skills at the 2.2 grade level (12th percentile)

Citing the background information and following assessments, choose three of Ramon's strengths and two of his major needs. Describe how the teacher will carry out some of your own the instruction to meet his needs.

*Kanon*

Graded Words in Isolation Test: Form A

## Grade 2

| | | Flashed | Delayed |
|---|---|---|---|
| 1. | low | | |
| 2. | deer | | |
| 3. | few | | |
| 4. | afraid | | |
| 5. | rest | | |
| 6. | mile | | |
| 7. | such | | |
| 8. | I'd | | |
| 9. | carry | | |
| 10. | puppy | | |
| 11. | owl | | |
| 12. | seven | | |
| 13. | quick | | |
| 14. | mountain | | |
| 15. | visit | | |
| 16. | follow | | |
| 17. | dragon | | |
| 18. | anyone | | |
| 19. | farmer | | |
| 20. | evening | | |

_____ %

## Grade 3

| | | Flashed | Delayed |
|---|---|---|---|
| 1. | crop | ✓ | |
| 2. | force | ✓ | |
| 3. | motor | ✓ | |
| 4. | usual | ✓ | |
| 5. | yesterday | | ✓ |
| 6. | bother | | ✓ |
| 7. | enjoy | ✓ | |
| 8. | history | ✓ | |
| 9. | nibble | ✓ | |
| 10. | scratch | ✓ | |
| 11. | parent | ✓ | |
| 12. | television | ✓ | |
| 13. | whisker | | ✓ |
| 14. | treat | ✓ | |
| 15. | accident | | ✓ |
| 16. | dare | — | — |
| 17. | understood | | ✓ |
| 18. | notebook | | ✓ |
| 19. | amaze | — | — |
| 20. | familiar | — | — |

_85_ %

From Ezra L. Stieglitz. *The Stieglitz Informal Reading Inventory.*
(Second Edition) Boston, Massachusetts: Allyn and Bacon 1997

Carson

Graded Reading Passages Test: Form D—Narrative 265

N *The Blind Woman* (3)

INTRODUCTION: Please read this story about a woman who could not see.

*The Blind Woman*

A woman who had become blind called a doctor. She promised that if he could cure her, she would reward (reword) him well. If he failed, he would get nothing. The doctor agreed.

He went often to the woman's apartment. He would pretend to treat her eyes. But he would also steal furniture (faniter) and other objects. Little by little, he took all her belongings. Finally, he used his skill to cure (care) her and asked for his money.

Every time he asked for his payment, the woman made up a reason for not paying him. Eventually he took her to court. The woman said to the judge, "I did promise to pay the doctor if he gave me back my sight. However, how can I be cured (Cared)? If I truly (dK) could see, wouldn't I see furniture (faniter) and other belongings in my house?"

**L - Literal**
**I - Inferential**

COMPREHENSION CHECK

| | | Probed Recall | Free Recall |
|---|---|---|---|
| L 1. | Who did the woman ask for help? (a doctor) | | ✓ |
| L 2. | What promise did the woman make to the doctor? (to pay him well only if he cured her) | ✓ | |
| L 3. | What did the doctor do while in the woman's apartment? (took furniture) (took all her belongings) | | ✓ |
| L 4. | Why did the doctor take the woman to court? (because he wanted his payment) | | ✓ |
| I 5. | Why didn't the woman want to pay the doctor for curing her blindness? (She felt he didn't deserve to be paid because he was a thief.) | X | |
| C 6. | What would you do if you were the judge in this case? (Accept any logical response, such as "I would place the doctor in jail for being dishonest.") | ✓ | |

Total Comprehension Errors 1 I (L & I)

Retell

A doctor promise a blind woman to make her see again. She promise to pay him. She not pay him because he took her stuff -- She say if she can see, where is her stuff?

From Ezra L. Stieglitz. *The Stieglitz Informal Reading Inventory*. (Second Edition) Boston, Massachusetts: Allyn and Bacon 1997

**Quick Write**

For I have 1 chah
to go a arawn the ward
I go to philipnes becouse
I born in philipnes and my
Parent born in philipner
and in philipnes is not very
cold and not very hot
and in the philipnes more rain
drown in the ground, plents,
trees, and ocean and in philipne
the peppole helping

**Final Draft**

for I have one chansh
to go arawnd the world I wilbo to
philipres becouse in the the air in the
the philipnes is not very cold and the
fruit is tyrish uff and the trees
of philipnes are taller and in the moning the
sun is beautiful and
the plents up and up and the rain
down in the rut of the tree and
I hir the bird singing in the trees
and the dogs are say raray, rora and raw,

and I feeling in the philipnes
I happy and the grass flowsrs tree
and ground are very bedtiful

and in the philipnes the rain is
beautiful see in the widows are in
dars and fruit of papay is good
in the philipnes and

Make some notes of your own before turning the page.

## Strengths

_____

_____

_____

_____

_____

_____

_____

_____

## Needs

_____

_____

_____

_____

_____

_____

_____

_____

## Strategies and Rationale

_____

_____

_____

_____

_____

_____

_____

_____

## Brainstorming Response Ideas

### Strengths

- Has mastered some word recognition and decoding skills at the third grade level
- Has good comprehension at the third grade level
- Can communicate in English in day-to-day interactions (pragmatics)
- Has self-knowledge about his strengths and weaknesses (metacognition)
- Knows two languages
- Has motivation to learn

### Needs

- Increased attention to endings in oral reading
- English language development
- Increased English vocabulary
- Understanding that the purpose for reading is to read for meaning and of the strategies that good readers use
- Confidence in reading
- More control over written language—syntax and the writing process

### Strategies and Rationale

- Read-alouds/think-alouds to model English language structure, fluency, and expression
- Before, During, and After comprehension strategies:
  - Share background knowledge, make predictions
  - Read in small chunks (paragraphs or single pages), and summarize and make personal connections, connections to the world, and other books.
  - Use context clues for new vocabulary.
  - Model monitoring—reread to clarify, ask questions throughout text to self, author check predictions (correct and confirm), visualize.
- Guided Reading group to practice strategies that were modeled
- For writing, help student see the connection between oral and written language; provide many writing samples; model writing in front of students, including paragraph organization, thinking aloud as the draft progresses; provide opportunities on a daily basis for student to write authentic pieces; through the editing process, teach grammatical structures and conventions based on those that confuse student—tenses, parallel structure, run-on sentences, use of capitals and punctuation; demonstrate proofreading for spelling.
- Writers' workshop framework

## Narrative

Ramon is a strong reader for an English language learner who has been in the United States for only a year. On his writing assessment, Ramon had a lot to say about his home, the Philippines, and although he shows his passion and his exuberance about the country he left, he still needs work on English language development in speaking and writing.

Ramon's strengths in reading are indicated by the Graded Words in Isolation Test and the third grade reading passage. In fact, the standardized test profile shows that he has made better-than-average progress in comprehension for a second language learner. The words in isolation that he was able to read on the test indicate that he has accumulated a set of third grade words that he recognizes instantly, and several multisyllabic words that he was able to decode. His informal reading passage shows strengths in many components of reading, such as a well-developed sight vocabulary and strong comprehension, as seen in his retelling and answers to the questions. Even though he missed the answer to the inferential question, Ramon shows a particular strength in making inferences in his retelling. He reveals his understanding of the story about the woman's comment to the judge: "She say, if she can see, where is her stuff?"

Ramon has two major needs on which his teacher should focus. The most obvious is his need to develop more control over English language syntax in both oral and written language. Although this issue did not affect his comprehension, he does omit word endings while reading aloud, which is common for English language learners.

So that Ramon becomes familiar with English syntax, his teacher should read aloud many high-quality books, and use think-aloud along with the reading. This strategy involves responding to the text while reading. For instance, the teacher will read a section of the text, and reveal what is going on in his/her mind to demonstrate what strategies a good reader uses to make sense of text. The type of strategies he/she might show are summarizing the section, making predictions, confirming or correcting predictions, asking questions of himself/herself or the author, visualizing, making connections to self (his/her background experience), connections with the world or other books, modeling the use of context clues, and other vocabulary strategies. If the teacher models this regularly, Ramon will have a better understanding of the reading process, and methods to handle unknown vocabulary. This understanding should carry over into his guided reading group where he can practice applying Before, During, and After comprehension strategies. In this way, Ramon will bring more meaning to text and build his confidence in reading and speaking. To prevent embarrassment, the teacher might also address his omission of word endings in the safety of the small, guided reading group or one-on-one.

In order to address his needs in writing, the teacher needs to help Ramon see the connection between oral and written language by providing many writing samples. His/her instruction should include modeling writing for Ramon, especially for paragraph organization, and thinking aloud as the draft progresses. He/she should also provide opportunities on a daily basis for him to write authentic pieces. Through the editing process, he/she should teach grammatical structures and conventions based on those that confuse Ramon, such as tenses, parallel structure, run-on sentences, the use of capitals, and punctuation. He/she should also teach proofreading, particularly for spelling. This instruction could take place within the framework of a writers' workshop.

# Domains I–IV
## Sixth Grade Individual

Madeline is a sixth grader who has fair word attack skills but lacks fluency, because she reads without expression and ignores punctuation. This issue interferes with her comprehension: she does not monitor what she reads. She is unable to retell a passage or answer questions on the various levels of understanding. Standardized test as well as individualized reading assessment scores show her word attack skills to be on the fourth grade level and her comprehension to be on the third grade level. Madeline is an avid viewer of educational television channels. This gives her the opportunity to absorb much information about history and science. In her textbooks, she relies heavily on picture cues, graphs, and charts, and uses her background knowledge to fill in the gaps. Therefore, she gets good grades in subjects such as science and social studies. Because of her extensive background knowledge, she is able to actively participate in some class discussions, but her ideas are not always pertinent to the book under discussion. She has a rich vocabulary that shows in her speech and writing. However, she does not read books for enjoyment.

Given this information and the sample below, give two examples of Madeline's strengths and two major needs. Describe instructional strategies that the teacher should use to address her needs, and offer some assessment practices to monitor her progress.

Madeline

The Human Skeleton has 206 Bones in the body.
Their joints help the bones move around.
Muscles give the bones flexibility.
There are about 602 muscles in the body.
The bones hold up the body by
providing structure.

Make some notes of your own before turning the page.

## Strengths

_____

_____

_____

_____

_____

_____

_____

_____

## Needs

_____

_____

_____

_____

_____

_____

_____

_____

## Strategies and Assessments

_____

_____

_____

_____

_____

_____

_____

_____

# Brainstorming Response Ideas

## Strengths
- Uses background knowledge
- Has some word attack skills
- Has fair amount of vocabulary knowledge
- Participates in discussions
- Uses visuals to comprehend textbooks
- Relates well to content material
- Absorbs information from other sources besides reading

## Needs
- To increase comprehension strategies
- To achieve fluency in reading
- To have more independent practice in reading
- To connect background knowledge and vocabulary to reading

# Instructional Strategies Recommended

## Comprehension Strategies for Narrative Text (Story Material)

In small groups, the whole class, or Literature Circles, model and coach Madeline to use the following:

### Before Reading (Into)
- Use background knowledge to make predictions about the story using the title.
- Have student select some key vocabulary to preview.
- Use vocabulary to confirm or correct previous predictions.
- Record student's predictions on board, on chart paper, or in student journal.
- In place of writing predictions, help student make a graphic organizer (semantic map, visual representation of ideas), using background knowledge to brainstorm ideas about setting—for instance, knowledge of the Holocaust and World War II for *The Diary of Anne Frank*.

### During Reading (Through)
- Do think-alouds (model how text sounds and how good readers construct meaning as they read).
- Set purpose for reading (to check predictions).
- Break down passage into manageable chunks.
- To teach monitoring of comprehension: Using reading response journals, have student note ideas, questions, and parts of the text that are confusing (add page numbers).
- Use reciprocal teaching (have student generate questions, clarify answers or ideas with partner, retell or summarize sequence of events to partner or group).
- Reread to apply fix-up strategies when confused.

### After Reading (Beyond)
- Use graphic organizers (semantic webs) to detail elements of literature (setting, characters, theme, conflict, and so on).
- Use questions to stimulate discussions that require literal, inferential, analytical, evaluative, and connective thinking (personal connections to story).
- Show student how to look back into text to support answers.
- Have student write reactions and responses in journals.
- Have student write descriptions in the style of the author or genre.

### Building Fluency and Independent Reading
■ Do "book talks" with student to stimulate interest in fiction.
■ Do creative dramatics to encourage fluency and expression.
■ Do teacher read-alouds to model fluency and expression (phrase reading in particular).
■ Provide many and different types of materials and genres from which student can choose.
■ Give alternative assignments to book reports to accommodate different learning style.

## Comprehension Strategies for Expository Material (Factual Text)

Using a small group or whole class, model and coach student to use the following:
■ Use the content area textbook and other reference material for locating and retrieving information, such as when:
  ■ Predicting
  ■ Previewing
  ■ Activating background knowledge
  ■ Organizing text (location of main idea in paragraphs, signal words, patterns in paragraphs)
■ Use the content area textbook and other reference material for retaining information, using strategies including:
  ■ Note taking
  ■ Outlining
  ■ Summarizing
  ■ Graphic organizers
  ■ Report writing
■ Strategies reflect techniques contained in SQ3R (Study, Question, Read, Recite, Review) and KWL (Know, Want to Know, Learn).

### Ongoing Assessment
■ Use periodic conferences and informal reading inventories (add retelling immediately following oral reading), and ask questions on various levels (literal, inferential, and critical thinking) to check on comprehension and monitoring.
■ Use teacher-made tests such as cloze procedure, essays, and performance assessments.
■ Analyze standardized testing to determine whether student is able to show what he or she knows on measures that are timed and require silent reading.

# Narrative

The evidence shows that Madeline has a major strength in the area of background knowledge that allows her to succeed in subjects like science and social studies. She also has a relative strength in word attack. Because of the word attack skills she has in place, Madeline does not struggle over every word. However, she does not really have fluency, and she has little comprehension.

For narrative text, Madeline's instruction should include Before reading strategies, such as activating background knowledge with semantic maps (graphic organizers), previewing, and making predictions. During reading, the teacher should model the use of think-alouds, as Madeline needs know how to read to check predictions, break down passages (chunking), and monitor comprehension by noting ideas in a reading response log as she goes along. Madeline also needs to be involved in reciprocal teaching to generate questions, clarify answers, summarize with a partner, and apply fix-up strategies when reading doesn't make sense. After reading, she needs to learn how to use semantic webs to detail elements of literature, and how to answer questions that require literal, inferential, analytical, evaluative, and connective thinking; she also needs to learn how to locate support for her answers in text, and to write responses in her journal.

For expository text, Madeline needs modeling of strategies for textbooks and reference material, such as predicting, previewing vocabulary and concepts, activating background knowledge (SQ3R or KWL), determining organization of text (location of main idea, signal words, patterns like comparison-contrast, cause-effect), note taking, outlining, summarizing, using graphic organizers, and writing reports.

In order to build reading fluency and independent reading, Madeline should hear book talks and participate in literature circles, be involved in creative dramatics, and listen to teacher read-alouds. The teacher might also assign alternative forms of book reports to stimulate interest in reading.

The teacher should periodically assess Madeline's progress by recording her oral readings and retellings and cloze procedure to check comprehension and monitoring strategies. Madeline also needs to learn self-assessment through developing a portfolio that includes the audiotapes of her reading and shows her growth over time. Standardized tests can be used to determine progress in silent, timed reading.

# References

Adams, M. 1994. *Beginning to Read: Thinking and Learning About Print.* Cambridge, Massachusetts: MIT Press.

Adams, M., Foorman, B. R., Lundberg, I., and Beeler, T. 1998. *Phonemic Awareness in Young Children.* Baltimore, Maryland: Paul H. Brookes Publishing Co.

Atwell, N. 1998. *In the Middle: New Understanding, About Writing, Reading and Learning.* 2nd ed. Portsmouth, New Hampshire: Boynton/Cook.

Atwell, N. 1989. *In the Middle: Writing, Reading, and Learning with Adolescents.* Portsmouth, New Hampshire: Boynton/Cook.

Bear, D., Invernizzi, M., Templeton, S., and Johnston, F. 2003. *Words Their Way: Word Study for Phonics, Vocabulary, and Spelling Instruction.* Englewood Cliffs, New Jersey: Prentice Hall.

Burns, P. C., Roe, B. D., and Ross, E. P. 1995. *Teaching Reading in Today's Elementary Schools.* Boston, Massachusetts: Houghton Mifflin.

California State Board of Education and California Commission for the Establishment of Academic Content and Performance Standards. *Language Arts: Reading, Writing, Listening, and Speaking Content Standards for Grades K–12.* Sacramento, California: California Department of Education.

Carnine, D. W., Silbert, J., Kame'enui, E. J., and Tarver, S. 2004. *Direct Instruction Reading,* 4th ed. Englewood Cliffs, New Jersey: Prentice Hall.

Clay, M. 1991. *Becoming Literate. The Construction of Inner Control.* Portsmouth, New Hampshire: Heinemann.

Cunningham, P. M. 2004. *Phonics They Use: Words for Reading and Writing,* 3rd ed. New York: HarperCollins.

Daniels, H. 2001. *Literature Circles: Voice and Choice in the Student-Centered Classroom.* 2nd ed. York, Maine: Stenhouse.

Fountas, I. C., and Pinnell, G. S. 1996. *Guided Reading: Good First Teaching for All Children.* Portsmouth, New Hampshire: Heinemann.

Graves, D. H. 1994. *A Fresh Look at Writing.* Portsmouth, New Hampshire: Heinemann.

*Graves, M. F., Juel, C., and Graves, B. B. 2003. *Teaching Reading in the 21st Century,* 3rd ed. Needham Heights, Massachusetts: Allyn & Bacon.

Gunning, T. G. 1998. *Assessing and Correcting Reading and Writing Difficulties.* Needham Heights, Massachusetts: Allyn & Bacon.

*Gunning, T. G. 2002. *Creating Reading Instruction for All Children,* 4th ed. Needham Heights, Massachusetts: Allyn & Bacon.

Henderson, E. H., and Beers, J. 1980. *Developmental and Cognitive Aspects of Learning to Spell.* Newark, Delaware: International Reading Association.

Lapp, D., Flood, J., and Farnan, N., eds. 2004. *Content Area Reading and Learning: Instructional Strategies*, 3rd ed. Needham Heights, Massachusetts: Allyn & Bacon.

*Peregoy, S., and Boyle, O. 2004. *Reading, Writing, and Learning in ESL: A Resource Book for K–12 Teachers*. White Plains, New York: Longman.

*Reutzel, D. R., and Cooter, Jr., R. B. 2003. *Teaching Children to Read: Putting the Pieces Together*, 3rd ed. Englewood Cliffs, New Jersey: Prentice Hall.

Richek, M. A., Schudt C. J., Holt J. J., and Lerner, J. W. 2001. *Reading Problems: Assessment and Teaching Strategies*. Needham Heights, Massachusetts: Allyn & Bacon.

*Ruddell, R. B. 2005. *Teaching Children to Read and Write: Becoming an Effective Literacy Teacher*, 3rd ed. Needham Heights, Massachusetts: Allyn & Bacon.

*Sampson, M., Sampson, M. B., and Van Allen, R. 1995. *Pathways to Literacy*. Fort Worth, Texas: Harcourt Brace College Publishers.

Samway, K. D., and Whang, G. 1995. *Literature Study Circles in a Multicultural Classroom*. York, Maine: Stenhouse.

Schipper, B., and Rossi, J. 1997. *Portfolios in the Classroom*. York, Maine: Stenhouse.

*Tompkins, G. E. 2005. *Literacy for the 21st Century: A Balanced Approach*, 4th ed. Englewood Cliffs, New Jersey: Prentice Hall.

Vacca, R. T., and Vacca, J. L. 2004. *Content Area Reading: Literacy and Learning Across the Curriculum*, 8th ed. New York: HarperCollins.

Yopp, H. K. 1992. "Developing Phonemic Awareness in Young Children." *The Reading Teacher*, 45, 696–703.

The titles that are starred* in the list of references are textbooks that cover in depth all components of reading.

The following texts are recommended for reference for their in-depth coverage of:

- ∎ Phonics and systematic phonics instruction
- ∎ Phonemic awareness
- ∎ Decodable text and predictable test

Adams, M. 1994. *Beginning to Read: Thinking and Learning About Print*. Cambridge, Massachusetts: MIT Press.

Adams, M., Foorman, B. R., Lundberg, I., and Beeler, T. 1998. *Phonemic Awareness in Young Children*. Baltimore, Maryland: Paul H. Brookes Publishing Co.

Atwell, N. 1989. *In the Middle: Writing, Reading, and Learning with Adolescents*. Portsmouth, New Hampshire: Boynton/Cook.

Bear, D., Invernizzi, M., Templeton, S., and Johnston, F. 2003. *Words Their Way: Word Study for Phonics, Vocabulary, and Spelling Instruction.* Englewood Cliffs, New Jersey: Prentice Hall.

Burns, P. C., Roe, B. D., and Ross, E. P. 1995. *Teaching Reading in Today's Elementary Schools.* Boston, Massachusetts: Houghton Mifflin.

Carnine, D. W., Silbert, J., Kame'enui, E. J., and Tarver, S. 2003. *Direct Instruction Reading,* 4th ed. Englewood Cliffs, New Jersey: Prentice Hall.

Clay, M. 1991. *Becoming Literate: The Construction of Inner Control.* Portsmouth, New Hampshire: Heinemann.

Cunningham, P. M. 2004. *Phonics They Use: Words for Reading and Writing,* 4th ed. New York: HarperCollins.

Fountas, I. C., and Pinnell, G. S. 1996. *Guided Reading: Good First Teaching for All Children.* Portsmouth, New Hampshire: Heinemann.

*Gunning, T. G. 1998. *Assessing and Correcting Reading and Writing Difficulties.* Needham Heights, Massachusetts: Allyn & Bacon.

Yopp, H. K. 1992. "Developing Phonemic Awareness in Young Children." *The Reading Teacher, 45,* 696–703.

# Comprehension and Comprehension Strategies

Brown, A. L. 1980. "Metacognitive Development and Reading." In R. J. Spiro, B. C. Bruce, and W. F. Brewer, eds. *Theoretical Issues in Reading Comprehension.* Hillsdale, New Jersey: Erlbaum.

Brown, H., and Cambourne, B. 1990. *Read and Retell.* Portsmouth, New Hampshire: Heinemann.

Clay, M. 1979. *The Early Detection of Reading Difficulties: A Diagnostic Survey with Recovery Procedures,* 2nd ed. Auckland, New Zealand: Heinemann.

Cudd, E. T., and Roberts, L. L. 1987. "Using Story Frames to Develop Reading Comprehension in a First Grade Classroom." *The Reading Teacher, 41*(1), 74–81.

Goodman, Y., and Burke, C. L. 1970. *Reading Miscue Manual Procedure for Diagnosis and Evaluation.* New York: Macmillan.

Graves, M. F., Juel, C., and Graves, B. B. 2003. *Teaching Reading in the 21st Century,* 3rd ed. Needham Heights, Massachusetts: Allyn & Bacon.

*Gunning, T. G. 1998. *Assessing and Correcting Reading and Writing Difficulties.* Needham Heights, Massachusetts: Allyn & Bacon.

*Gunning, T. G. 2002. *Creating Reading Instruction for All Children,* 4th ed. Needham Heights, Massachusetts: Allyn & Bacon.

Meeks, J. W., and Morgan, R. F. 1978. "Classroom and the Cloze Procedure: Interaction in Imagery." *Reading Horizons, 18,* 261–264.

Nist, S. L., and Kirby, K. 1986. "Teaching Comprehension and Study Strategies Through Modeling and Thinking Aloud." *Reading Research and Instruction, 25,* 254–264.

Ogle, D. 1992. "KWL in Action: Secondary Teachers Find Applications That Work." In E. K. Dishner, T. W. Bean, J. E. Readance, and D. W. Moore, eds. *Content Area Reading: Improving Classroom Instruction*, 3rd ed. Dubuque, Iowa: Kendall/Hunt.

Reutzel, D. R., and Cooter, Jr., R. B. 2003. *Teaching Children to Read: Putting the Pieces Together*, 3rd ed. Englewood Cliffs, New Jersey: Prentice Hall.

*Ruddell, R. B. 2005. *Teaching Children to Read and Write: Becoming an Effective Literacy Teacher*, 3rd ed. Needham Heights, Massachusetts: Allyn & Bacon.

# Writing, Interactive Writing, Conferences, Writing Process

Atwell, N. 1987. *In the Middle: Writing, Reading, and Learning with Adolescents*. Portsmouth, New Hampshire: Boynton/Cook.

*Graves, D. H. 1994. *A Fresh Look at Writing*. Portsmouth, New Hampshire: Heinemann.

*Gunning, T. G. 1998. *Assessing and Correcting Reading and Writing Difficulties*. Needham Heights, Massachusetts: Allyn & Bacon.

Tompkins, G. E. 2005. *Literacy in the 21st Century: A Balanced Approach*. Englewood Cliffs, New Jersey: Prentice Hall.

# Assessment, Miscue Analysis, Running Records, Retellings, Portfolios, Cloze Procedure

Brown, H., and Cambourne, B. 1990. *Read and Retell*. Portsmouth, New Hampshire: Heinemann.

Burns, P. C., and Roe, B. D. 2001. *Informal Reading Inventory: Preprimer to Twelfth Grade*. Boston, Massachusetts: Houghton Mifflin.

Clay, M. 2002. *An Observation Survey of Early Literacy Achievement*. Portsmouth, New Hampshire: Heinemann.

Farr, R., and Tone, B. 1998. *Portfolios and Performance Assessment*. Orlando, Florida: Harcourt Brace.

*Fountas, I. C., and Pinnell, G. S. 1996. *Guided Reading: Good First Teaching for All Children*. Portsmouth, New Hampshire: Heinemann.

*Gunning, T. G. 1998. *Assessing and Correcting Reading and Writing Difficulties*. Needham Heights, Massachusetts: Allyn & Bacon.

*The Primary Language Record*. 1989. London, England: Center for Language in Primary Education. Also published by Heinemann Educational Books, Portsmouth, New Hampshire.

Richek, M. A., Schudt Caldwell, J., Holt Jennings, J., and Lerner, J. W. 1996. *Reading Problems: Assessment and Teaching Strategies*. Needham Heights, Massachusetts: Allyn & Bacon.

Schipper, B., and Rossi, J. 1997. *Portfolios in the Classroom*. York, Maine: Stenhouse.

Stieglitz, E. L. 2001. *The Stieglitz Informal Reading Inventory*, 2nd ed. Needham Heights, Massachusetts: Allyn & Bacon.

## Study Skills; Prereading Strategies; Before, During, and After Reading Strategies; Expository and Narrative Text Structure

Graves, M. F., Juel, C., and Graves, B. B. 2003. *Teaching Reading in the 21st Century*, 3rd ed. Needham Heights, Massachusetts: Allyn & Bacon.

Lapp, D., Flood, J., and Farnan, N., eds. 2004. *Content Area Reading and Learning: Instructional Strategies*, 3rd ed. Needham Heights, Massachussetts: Allyn & Bacon.

Robinson, R. P. 1941. *Effective Study*. New York: Harper and Row.

Vacca, R. T., and Vacca, J. L. 2004. *Content Area Reading: Literacy and Learning Across the Curriculum*, 8th ed. New York: HarperCollins.

Yopp, R. H., and Yopp, H. K. 1992. *Literature-Based Reading Activities*. Needham Heights, Massachusetts: Allyn & Bacon.

## English as a Second Language

Peregoy, S., and Boyle, O. 2004. *Reading, Writing, and Learning in ESL: A Resource Book for K–12 Teachers*. White Plains, New York: Longman.

Richard-Amato, P. A., and Snow, M. A. 1992. *The Multicultural Classroom: Readings for Content Area Teachers*. Reading, Massachusetts: Addison-Wesley.

## Literature Circles

Campbell-Hill, B., Johnson, N. J., and Schick-Noe, K. L. 1995. *Literature Circles and Response*. Norwood, Massachusetts: Christopher-Gordon.

Daniels, H. 2001. *Literature Circles: Voice and Choice in the Student-Centered Classroom*, 2nd ed. York, Maine: Stenhouse.

Samway, K. D., and Whang, G. 1995. *Literature Study Circles in a Multicultural Classroom*. York, Maine: Stenhouse.

## Spelling, Vocabulary

Cunningham, P. M. 2004. *Phonics They Use: Words for Reading and Writing*, 4th ed. New York: HarperCollins.

Henderson, E. H., and Beers, J. 1980. *Developmental and Cognitive Aspects of Learning to Spell*. Newark, Delaware. International Reading Association.

Richek, M. A., Schudt, C. J., Holt, J. J., and Lerner, J. W. 2001. *Reading Problems: Assessment and Teaching Strategies*. Needham Heights, Massachusetts: Allyn & Bacon.

# Master List of Terms

**Anecdotal records**
**Assessment**: Running records, miscue analysis, informal reading inventories
**Baseline information**
**Benchmarks and developmental milestones**: Observational checklist
**Cloze procedure**
**Comprehension**: Literal, main idea, inferential, critical thinking
**Comprehension strategies**: Self-monitoring, self-correcting, rereading, summarizing, asking questions, clarifying, synthesizing
**Concepts of print**
**Conferences**
**Cue systems**: Semantic, syntactic, and graphophonic or graphophonemic
**Decodable text, predictable test**
**Differentiated instruction**
**Environmental print**
**Expository text structure**: Simple list/description, time/order, comparison/contrast, cause/effect
**Flexible grouping**
**Genres**
**Guided reading**
**Implicit instruction**
**Interactive writing/shared writing/shared pen**
**Language experience approach**
**Learning logs/reading response journals**
**Listening samples**
**Literature circles**
**Mapping**
**Narrative text structure**: Elements of literature (character, plot, setting, conflict, climax, resolution, figurative language, similes, metaphors, mood, tone, foreshadowing, flashback, protagonist, antagonist)
**Onsets and rimes**
**Oral cloze**
**Oral language development**
**Phonemic awareness**: Rhyming, blending, segmenting, substitution
**Phonics and systematic, explicit phonics instruction/embedded or implicit**: phonemes, morphemes, consonants, vowels, blends, digraphs, diphthongs

**Portfolios**
**Pre-reading strategies, Before-During-After strategies (Into, Through, Beyond)**
**Question, Answer Relationship (QAR)**
**Readers' theatre**
**Readers' workshop**
**Reciprocal teaching**
**Retelling**
**Study skill strategies**: SQ3R, graphic organizers, KWL, summarizing, note taking, outlining
**Think-aloud**
**VAKT (Visual, Auditory, Kinesthetic, Tactile)**
**Vocabulary**
**Word analysis**
**Word walls**
**Writer's workshop**